Obedience to Reality

ELOROS Studies 1

Obedience to Reality

Essays on Religious Life

Eloise Rosenblatt, R.S.M.

WestWind Press
North Richland Hills, Texas

WestWind Press
An imprint of D. & F. Scott Publishing, Inc.
P.O. Box 821653
N. Richland Hills, TX 76182
817 788-2280
info@dfscott.com
www.dfscott.com

Printed in the United States of America

10 09 08 07 06   5 4 3 2 1

Library of Congress Cataloging-in-Publication Data
Rosenblatt, Marie Eloise.
  Obedience to reality : essays on religious life / Eloise Rosenblatt.
    p. cm. -- (ELOROS studies ; 1)
  Summary: "Essays on religious life of nuns by a sister of the Sisters of
Mercy"--Provided by publisher.
  ISBN 1-930566-57-3 (trade paper : alk. paper)
  1. Monastic and religious life of women. 2. Sisters of Mercy. I. Title. II.
Series.
  BX4210.R66 2006
  255'.9--dc22
                                    2006015021

Front cover image by arrangement with www.clipart.com: *Woman of Samaria
at Well*, by Lavinia Fontana (1552-1614), a female artist of the Italian Renais-
sance who, among other honors, was a portraitist at the court of Pope Paul V.
She was best known for receiving a papal commission from Pope Clement VIII
for an extremely large altarpiece for the basilica of S Paolo fuori le Mura. This
magnificent altarpiece, that stood over twenty feet tall, was named *The Ston-
ing of Saint Stephen Martyr.* She is famous for making the largest body of work
produced by a female artist before 1700. She created 135 documented paint-
ings, of which thirty are known to have survived. *Woman of Samaria at Well* is
in the Museo di Capodimonte at Naples, Italy.

In Memory of Sister Mary Roqueta Zappia, R.S.M.

1915–2005

"The problem is power and authority,
authority and power."

Contents

Preface

Jesus advises his disciples against making displays of their piety, and instead counsels, "Go into your room, shut the door, and pray to your Father who is in secret, and your Father who sees in secret will reward you." (Matt 6:5–6)

When I was in the novitiate in 1969, I read a one-line reference to a Sister-author who took this counsel to heart not only about her prayer, but her writing. In one of those many solid tomes of spiritual theology on convent shelves, most of them written by male theologians, one had the line, "Translated by a Nun of Standbrook Abbey." I found this English monastic woman's anonymity so puzzling that I have never forgotten the inscription. Why would a writer, because she was a nun, draw a cloak over her own face, when the male author of this volume didn't conceal his identity?

It is not so long since those novitiate days. A generation later, more women write and publish under their own names. But in the world of theology and spirituality, women still feel their assignment to accept silence and self-effacement as greater virtues than writing and publishing as identified authors. There are exceptions, but the number of vowed women writers is not at all proportional to their potential, since there are roughly three times more Sisters than male religious, whose publications flourish. Adding to the paradox, more women today have advanced academic degrees in theology and related disciplines than forty years ago. They are able to write.

Nevertheless, religious culture still assigns women the greater share of working at the virtues of long-suffering and humility. This is true in the west, and even more in Muslim theocracies of the east. The instinct of enlightened women is that the culture that rewards and reinforces women's silence must be resisted if there is to be justice for the poor. Those who do not speak, or have no one to speak for them, remain the oppressed and victimized. While I always understood academic publishing as a political act to advance one's professional career, theological publishing by women is not career-oriented, but an act that promotes justice and diminishes violence for women as a class. Publishing is speaking in public and engaging in conversation as a participant. As the philosophers of language insist, the goal is to be a "subject," speaking one's own truth, rather than an "object" whose reality and experience others describe.

Publishing resists the culture's assumption that women should or will accept any treatment they receive, from individuals or from political structures, in silent submission. The ethical perspective of women must be communicated and their flow of thought needs to be sustained as an abiding record of what women want for themselves and the world. This is also true for women in religious communities. Theological writing memorializes women's self-expression as a subject, and their enduring vision and values.

I have sustained a long commitment to promote the voice of religious women, especially Sisters of Mercy, my own sisterhood, through encouraging them to write and editing their texts for publication. In this volume, I am making an effort to follow the advice I give others—trust that what you have already written is worth retrieving and worth publishing. As for writing on scripture, theology, spirituality, and some legal themes, I have published a good deal for academic and popular audiences in my history as a university academic.

However, in recent months, I realized that a full body of writing done over the years still lay "in secret," accumulating in ever fuller file boxes. It became time to let these works see the light of day, if only to add my voice to the sound other women are making and increase volume so the impact of all of us may be stronger within Church and society.

This first volume of ELOROS Studies contains writings on religious life. I have a number of other writings on the same theme than those presented here, but let these suffice. While these essays all arise out of a particular occasion at a particular time, none of them has previously been published for a public other than the original hearers or readers, some of them very small groups.

I wrote "Obedience to Reality" in 1983 after an invitation to give a conference for Sisters of Mercy in Burlingame, California who were preparing for profession of vows. My instinct was to acknowledge the theology and spirituality of the vow, and also to probe what obedience might mean for any human being, and develop the sense of obedience as fidelity to one's own life-questions.

"The Mission of the Unpartnered Woman" of May 25, 1990 was presented as an address to a Provincial Assembly of the Sisters of Bon Secours in Marriottsville, Maryland. I gave a sequence of addresses to this dedicated and visionary community whose main work is health-care sponsorship.

The other essays arose *sua sponte*, or "from her own initiative," a legal phrase which describes the prerogative of a judge to initiate action from the bench without waiting for the lawyers in a case to first make a motion or objection. By this analogy, I would call these other essays *sua sponte*, or my spontaneous responses to the moment rather than direct invitations.

"Initiatives for the Burlingame Chapter" were presented to the regional community's steering committee in November, 2002. Not all the proposals were selected for discussion at the chapter of affairs or assembly at which formal congregational business was discussed and voted on. Of those selected, the order of presentation was determined by the logic of the business agenda. My effort in making short introductions for proposals, not provided in this volume, was to accomplish three goals: 1) to interpret the practical effects of the Institute Constitutions, the 1991 document that I believed had not yet been fully implemented; 2) to present the Church's official teaching about our ecclesial rights; and 3) to "plant seeds" for future action. None of the proposals was formally adopted by vote at that particular chapter. Presented here are the initiatives in their original sequence.

"Survey of Challenges for Orienting Mercy's Reconciliation Board" was prepared as background material for six members of a subcommittee of the Institute's Commission on Women in/of the Church meeting on June 6, 2004 in Chicago, headed by Helen

Marie Burns, R.S.M., vice-president of the Institute of the Sisters of Mercy. The purpose of this meeting was to plan for a gathering that eventually took place in March, 2005 in Detroit. The focus of the Detroit in-service was an orientation to the rights of members. The audience included representatives from regional community Reconciliation Boards. However, this particular document was not distributed to attendees.

"Comments on 'With a Passion for Christ and Passion for Humanity' the Working Paper for the Congress on Religious Life," was written in late November, 2004. It was a response to a posting of the paper at the website www.vidimusdominum.org (We have seen the Lord) in preparation for a meeting in Rome of the International Union of Superiors General of men's and women's religious orders (UISG). The website presented the draft in English, French, German, Spanish, and Italian. The theme of the conference focused on two scripture passages as metaphors of religious life: the Samaritan Woman (John 4:1–42) and the Good Samaritan (Luke 10:25–37). During the conference, there was a multilingual posting of papers by presenters and respondents, an altogether marvelous experience of accessibility to religious throughout the world. I sent my own Comments to an address for posting at the site. There was no acknowledgment of anyone receiving or reading it; only the consolation that it did not bounce back!

"Exploring the Civil and Canonical Rights of Sisters" is presented in a question-comment format. On December 10, 2004, I received a set of questions about the rights of religious women forwarded to me for comment from a posting to www.justiceforpriests.org. No author was given. I was so intrigued and absorbed by the quality of the questions, which struck me as unusually perceptive, that I hammered out an initial reflection on their worth, and outlined the sort of conversation that would be needed to answer them, six or seven pages of e-mail, as it turned out. As I later discovered, the author of the questions was Mary Therese Sweeney, C.S.J., a member of the leadership council of the Sisters of St. Joseph of Orange in southern California. This essay rearranges my comments under Mary Therese's original questions, and should be considered as a dialogue between women religious seeking to break new ground.

"Why an Appeals Process is Important for Our West-Midwest Governance Model" of December 15, 2005, was at attempt to push forward the ideas that I had addressed earlier in "Survey of Challenges for Orienting Mercy's Reconciliation Board." The Institute Constitutions of 1991 encodes several review processes that have not yet been practically or formally translated into any congregational governance structure because there is no conceptual basis for what "appeal" means in women's experience of religious life. Very few religious have practical experience of what it means to appeal a decision by someone in leadership and have it subjected to a review process. Obedience has erroneously been interpreted as the gospel counsel which overrides justice and any claim on one's most basic human rights.

My writings have not been "translated by a Nun of Standbrook Abbey," but may require their own translation into a language understood by present readers. I am confident that, like newer music or artwork, some alien-sounding writings may become less strange over time because they turn out to express the vision readers have carried without being fully aware of it. That remains my hope for the concept of religious women's rights in the Church.

As a final encouragement to other women writers, I urge you to remember that if the women who followed Jesus had not talked about their experience to other women first, and then to the male disciples, the Church would not have received the vision of Easter.

Easter
April 17, 2006

Obedience to Reality
Grounding, Testing, Living,
Working, and Imaging

I n speaking with you as you prepare for your Profession, I would like to propose that we consider the vow of obedience as obedience most fundamentally to reality; and our vow as expressing our sacred decision to make the realities of our life an ever more conscious reference point.

I am presupposing that you have dealt with the theological, scriptural, and religious life languages and concepts for talking about obedience. You understand obedience in religious life as a special act of consecration of your lives to God within the context of this community's mission and the larger frame of the Church's mission. I'm taking for granted that we see obedience as a way of talking about imitation of Jesus and living the gospel.

Grounding Obedience

When we consider the vow of obedience in relation to religious community, obedience becomes a way of describing our communal relationship to one another, and our relationship to the Church, and dedication of our energies to tasks too big for one person to do alone.

Obedience is a way to affirm our connection with this particular group, which is our spiritual center and social base. We speak of obedience as listening, openness, attention, responsiveness, or response-ability to something within and outside ourselves.

We link obedience to the achievement of freedom. And we consider obedience as inclusive of those to whom we are obedient, the persons in authority who serve us by exercising leadership—both in the Church and in our community. Obedience is the way we live our interdependence on one another. As we know from experience, love has to be the root of our lives, a human, warm affection, the sort of willingness to live "in love" with one another.

We can only enter into this marriage called community life for reasons of love. Love motivates us—not love for God and tolerance for one another, but love that is choice. This is not necessarily the romantic feelings that get it started. Without love, life together becomes that torture Sartre described in the drama *No Exit*: "Hell—it is the other people, the people around us." Without love we make no adjustments. There is no real reason to adjust our ideas, change ourselves, feel sensitive or sorry, or make sacrifices.

Without this affection, our listening, caring, changing, or adjusting are nothing but "should's" and we feel little but obligations that finally turn to resentment, estrangement, and entrenchment in our own perspective, interests, and lives. But with love, what a difference! Then it is the "Paradiso" of Dante's *Divine Comedy*, where he finds himself in canto five greeted by the blessed souls who make him welcome, "Look, here comes someone who will increase our love! Here comes one who makes our joy glow all the brighter!" This is how we could welcome one another in community.

It may be useful for our reflection to remember that a significant part of anyone's life involves obedience—obedience to others within a social or work structure. A community of love may or may not be involved, but structurally, we are constantly facing realities we didn't invent, but in which we operate. Soldiers know this, as do secretaries, doctors, nurses, social workers, factory laborers, environmentalists, politicians, executives, and scientists.

Even those who don't work, the retired and unemployed, know all about the system. Life becomes an art of operating in the system and surviving in it, and with good luck, we make it work for us. But we know many who feel the opposite. The system is their enemy; it crushes and kills them. The system, imperious and powerful, asserts itself.

But sometimes this assertion is for the good. Part of the restoration-of-health program for emotionally ill people is the restructuring of their environment by clear rules and procedures. Patients practice a kind of "obedience to the system." This operation within an external order helps some to recover an inner order, healing the interior disorder, calming the inner chaos, so that they can take charge of themselves again. Part of our own balance and sanity, our "being right with the world" is recognition of the structures and systems all around us.

In some mysterious way, Job experienced this as God's "answer" to his anguished question, "God, how is it just that good people like myself endure such hideous pain and loneliness?" God's "answer" has something to do with Job's confrontation with the system and structure of creation more immense than his imagination: "Here is the universe in all its beauty and majesty and you are within it and I am its creator and sustainer."

Another way to get at this idea that we are in systems whether we like it or not, whether we are in religious life or not, is recalling an adolescent's angry challenge to parents, "Well, I didn't ask to be born! So why should I have to do what you say?" We know what a parent's response is: "That's the way it is, kid. I'm the parent. You're my kid. You're here in the flesh." Someone always has power over us by virtue of age, precedence, physical strength, election, or economics. Maybe this is one advantage in being the youngest in a family: one comes more quickly to this truth than the eldest child, who can live longer under the illusion that the givens of life are negotiable. But this basic reality of the system is an inescapable *factum* of our lives, wherever we live it out.

Rather than belabor this point, which is what I mean by "grounding obedience," let's turn to what I mean by testing obedience.

Testing Obedience

Testing means trying something out, proving it, pushing at it to see for oneself what's there. An image that comes to mind is a blind man who taps with his stick to "see" or feel where the walls and edges, turns and blocks are to his movement. Part of obedience involves doing that sort of thing with the realities of our lives. Where are my limits? What do I have to do? What do I have some choices about? Where is my way clear?

I am not speaking of "stages." God deliver us from another model built on stages, even though they can be so convenient for pulling ideas into some kind of order. Our human experience always retains close affinity with the stuff of our making—chaos, formlessness, indeterminate matter, unanimated thing-ness. So let us not pretend that testing is the "next stage" after grounding obedience in reality. We are never done with testing.

What do I test? Sometimes we use and abuse the word "discernment" to describe this dynamic of testing. I test something if I'm not sure or clear enough to act without reservation. If I don't know whether it's a wall or a doorway in front of me, I stick out my hand or extend my stick. I test things out when I don't yet know my own mind.

Do I have a vocation to religious life or not? Do I love this man enough to marry him? Is this friendship where I want it to be? Is this work suited to my talents, the needs of the Church, the focus of the community in its present stage of self-definition and description? What do I really want? Is there something real here, or some sort of illusion or projection? Is something objective really there, or is it my imagination or my shadow leaping out at me? Testing involves dialogue with others when it's a matter of perceiving accurately.

But some things aren't a matter of perception so much as of acceptance. I discover I have a long-term illness and I must deal with this reality, not by daydreaming about its real or unreal existence, but by rearranging my life around the present inescapable facts. Likewise, when someone I love dies, when friendship turns to suspicion and I am rejected, or my marriage falls apart, the facts are usually pretty clear. So I face grief, separation, fear, wishing it were different. But nonetheless I accept, and don't deny the reality.

Jesus did this testing all his life. "Where are the possibilities, where are the limits, what do I have no choice but to accept? Will another miracle simply buy me time instead of giving me what is real and inescapable?" Facing and accepting death is the ultimate moment of testing reality and experiencing its limits for us in the time and space we know as "this world." Like Jesus, we face certain inevitabilities. Like him, we may find ourselves wedged in and crushed by the very systems, political and religious, which we have probed and poked at to determine their boundaries and our possibilities within them.

Testing reality confronts us with the wall, the "No Exit" or "Not a Through Street" signs, but also makes evident the vast realms where no limit impinges on us—the Grand Canyons and Big Sur horizons of life. And what freedom obedience to reality offers us here!

Testing is experiencing not only the walls, but discovering there aren't any walls where we thought there were. The Great Wall of China in our brain is only there, not in the system of religious life. Or the great Wall is in China, but not here where I am. These discoveries are just as much part of obedience as a No on a request for community funds to take a Caribbean pleasure cruise.

Living Obedience to Reality

The ideal of having predictability of people's actions to preserve peace and order in large groups may have been the undergirding for previous religious practices that were misnamed as expressions of obedience. A desert father tells an initiate to go plant cabbages upside down, and the obedience of the young brother in carrying out the directive without question is celebrated. He has given up his own will, along with his common sense. Pachomius, Basil, and Benedict wrote rules that ended up being obeyed in every prescription, from what to eat and when, to what prayers to say and when, to the order for turning in tools after a day of work.

Teresa of Avila, in her *Foundations*, records that her dear friend Maria de San Jose, prioress at Seville, was concerned that her Sisters were *too* obedient. She told Teresa she had to be careful not to joke about a Sister going to throw herself into a pond, because the Sister was likely to take her seriously—so literally did she regard her superior's merest suggestion. Like the prioress, we can see this exaggerated compliance as an inadequate and dehumanizing notion of obedience. Maybe things started as a wise person "making up" situations to test an initiate's ability to deal with reality if the reality were represented by a silly command, a hypothetical. Was the original point to have the initiate deal more with reality than with the literal content of the directive?

What may have been a teaching device to bring an initiate to a sense of non-negotiable reality ended up regarded by subsequent generations not as a teaching device, but as literal, fixated rules and practices around which a fantastic theology grew up to reinforce the rules and practices instead of the testing of reality.

Another abuse in the history of the development of religious obedience was a confusion between rule as guide for growth in love, and rule as management manual for a large community of unruly men of various ages. When you read the early rules, they are very much like an archdiocesan handbook, or a manual of policies to cover breaches of discipline. They make clear for large groups of people living together what shall be the common procedure for doing things like eating, working, praying, and selling goods for the community's livelihood.

Today we are still confused. Policy statements are management directives for large groups of us, to simplify our lives. Procedures are part of our reality, but following them should not be spiritualized, theologized, or scripturalized simply because they are guidelines for group order in a community of women. Everyone lives in a system, including us.

We are well aware that there is a difference between effective management and spiritual leadership, though in the past we may have suffered from the idiosyncrasies and caprices of religious superiors who identified the two. I am reluctant to identify compliance with the style of a superior with obedience to reality. I think there may have been an abuse of theology when we reinforced compliance with a superior's personal preferences as an essential part of our vocation to accept the Cross in our lives. This sort of compliance kept us from facing essential realities, and from discovering what the Cross was to be for us, the Cross, which is both negation and possibility.

This sort of obedience actually kept us from testing the great realities of life: the difference between illusion and existence, between dream as phantom and dream as awakening, between projection and ownership of feelings. Instead of gaining strength in discovering our own mind, we delivered ourselves up to the discernment of others. We never found out what our own questions were as distinct from theirs, or our own imperatives as distinct from those of the horarium.

Why did this mindless compliance go on for so long? Perhaps because conformity is easier than obedience to reality, the obedience that involves testing, proving, probing, trying, searching, and discerning reality for ourselves. If we are to move out of the stabilization period and through the breakdown and on to re-creation, we must assume responsibility for testing reality and in this way become more obedient than we were before.

Testing allows me to experience more freedom, not less. Without testing, I cannot live obedience. If I know where the rocks are, I can navigate my course through the channel more confidently, but I have to find out first. Otherwise, exercising my freedom is irresponsible and destructive to others. Frankel's thesis in *Logotherapy* was that we always have a choice about our attitude, even if we are destined for death in a concentration camp. To exercise that kind of freedom, I have to have tested my reality, and know that I am in a concentration camp, not wandering around Europe on a Eurail Pass. When I know well what my limits and possibilities are, I can begin living obedience to reality, acting on choices that are my own, choices that respect and acknowledge the systems I am in, both the ones I have chosen to live in, and the ones I don't have a choice about.

By living obedience to reality, I grow more deeply obedient, not less obedient. Living out of my own choices, however, can be scary, lonely, naked-feeling. How I wish sometimes to suit up in someone else's issues, or identify myself with some good cause because it's fashionable and approved. Then my obedience metamorphoses into unreflective conformity and unreality of the same order as following the horarium and calling myself obedient principally because I adhere to daily practices.

Obedience can include adherence to certain practices, but obedience to reality is the truer context for living obediently. I don't think living obedience is necessarily secure and comforting. I can try to rebuild security by assigning myself the task of answering someone else's questions, adopting someone else's issues, or defining myself by new structures. I can live my life as though I were filling out a civil service exam questionnaire: a comprehensive task, arduous, engrossing, but nevertheless someone else's questions.

Obedience that is living reality means finally, that we find out our own questions, and perhaps the issues that are right find us. We get seized like the prophets, captured, and just have to live in a particular way, out of certain convictions that grow from answers we are living to the unsolved questions that exist because we have discovered, from testing reality, where the definitive No's are, where the Yes's are, and all the provinces of Maybe's.

Living obedience is a release of energy, a fire in the bones, a jaw gritted determinedly. We live our gifts; we are faithful to our choice not to marry, to this moment in our community's history, to these possibilities for our ministry in the Church. We do not have absolute certainty, of course. Perhaps the only difference between testing and living obedience to reality is the degree of sureness. When we are living it, we are a little more sure than when we were testing it.

The Working of Obedience

This is what happened, I believe, to Jesus in the desert: He found himself ready to live obedience. His testing by the Evil One can be interpreted, on one level, as his testing of reality. From the testing emerged clarity of identity, self-direction, focused decision, and mission. Now he knew what he was hearing his Father say. He was attuned to the transcendent reality of his life as it affected his decision about what to do with his questions, convictions, and concerns. The release of energy was confirmed by the whole record of the public ministry—vigorous activity, powerful effects, his world exploding open as he realized his mission.

The description of testing and living obedience may sound a bit ideal. Paradoxically, we see religious around us who, despite having engaged in practices that seem alien today, their long observance of the rules of the horarium, and decades of conformity to the system—seem liberated as persons, spontaneous as individuals, loving and affectionate, balanced and open. Maybe not all of our Sisters, but enough for us to conclude that living something greater than the rule, being faithful to something greater than the system's limits and possibilities, has brought them to whatever real obedience was meant to be for.

If we are honest, we also have to say some religious got shot down as they tried to live this same obedience to reality. We may have seen them die on the field, as it were. They left religious life. We know some of the battle survivors who are walking around with shrapnel lodged in their hearts. We know some are still hiding out in the trenches, sure the enemy is still out there waiting to get them, and they prefer life in an emotional foxhole to the risk of any more testing or living obedience.

The appeal of obedience as true freedom sounds spiritually appealing. For high school students, being free of authority is the great ideal, the illusion that true individuality means "flying free" above the discipline of parents and teachers. But I understand living obedience as harder work than mere release from the disciplinary control of authority figures. The hard work of living obediently involves facing conflict, reversal, and opposition.

This is the obedience of Jesus in John's gospel: work, hard work, one long drama of protagonist against a succession of antagonists, scene after scene of Jesus on trial, facing a hostile jury, an inimical body of prosecutors. The system of religious and political forces was not alien to Jesus' experience. This is the system where he was grounded, the one he had tested, the one in which he lived. This was one of the elements of Jesus' reality: the system's effects were not what he chose, but the system was the only one in which he could authentically act.

After a day's hard work, we experience fatigue. We know what signs to recognize as the signals of burnout. Nothing is more exhausting than fighting City Hall and dealing with conflict situations in our home or work settings. The miracle of Jesus' compassion is not so much his responsiveness to sufferers, to the sick, the outcast and the desperate, but the fact that opposition and conflict didn't dry up his flow of love.

Some deep generative power in him, some grounding in love showed itself both in times of conflict as well as in times of acceptance. Whatever the exigencies of the system, something in Jesus could not be repressed. The power of love, presence and conviction in Jesus is comparable to those same forces that girded row upon row of striking Indians, followers of Gandhi, as they pressed forward to receive their inevitable beating by British soldiers. This is something of what I mean by obedience as working.

Working also meant, in the case of Jesus, that he produced change. When he was around, something happened. Structures were rattled, the system was challenged, customs bypassed, the helpless and victimized defended, the lives of his closest followers radically redirected and charged in a new way. The sick became well, apathy turned to enthusiasm, and death got cheated several times. On the other hand, support turned to hostility, trust to suspicion, interest to indifference. Jesus did get results, though not all the ones he would have chosen.

Obedience to reality pushes us into work of some sort, productive work, hard work, work that spends us, pours us out, stresses us. The work comes not because we are workaholics or have no life of friendship to nurture and support us. Work is an inevitability of our grounding, testing, and living.

There are a number of theological words we can use for this: ministry, apostolate, mission. I prefer to speak of Anglo-Saxon "work," something less exalted and closer to the ground, closer to our grounding. Our work is what we have to show for ourselves. Work is dignifying. But there is such a difference between the work "we are sent to do," as an assignment, as an expression of the community's mission, and that work that flows from the inner necessity of conviction, question or struggle. This is work that is an inevitability for us precisely because we are so obedient to our reality and the reality of the system of our community setting and the reality of the systems that surround those we know.

An Image of Obedience

Let me conclude these reflections on obedience to reality with the fragment of story that you may interpret as a kind of parable.

Three men set out from a village in southern Spain during spring of one year to join the pilgrimage leaving from Toledo for the Holy Land. One man was a *converso*, not of Old Catholic stock, and the Inquisition had made his pilgrimage to the shrines of Christendom the condition for his right to pass on his inheritance to his sons. He had to prove that he was united with the Catholic community of faith. Another was a man who had had devious dealings with cloth merchants in one province and upped the prices in his own province. His fraud had been discovered, and as a penance he was assigned the making of the pilgrimage as condition for his absolution. The third man was a devout Old Catholic. To fulfill a vow made when he prayed for his son's recovery, he was making the pilgrimage out of grateful devotion. The *converso*, a man experienced in forest paths, carried the compass. All carried walking sticks and food, together with knives and small tools for cutting wood needed for fire building and shelter making.

By day, they relied on the experience of the *converso* and his compass to set their direction. By night, the stars confirmed the direction the compass pointed out by day. Their aim, of course, was to join the larger company at Toledo whose guides, experienced in the long-distance routes, would lead them to their sacred destination and back home again.

The route through the forest was not easy. Recent snows made it necessary for them to test depressions to see if solid ground was underneath. They used their sticks to test the snow level, and when they were lucky to find caves between the rocks, they used their sticks to make sure the inside was free of snakes and animals so they could take shelter there. Frequently, their sticks assured them the path was clear, and they could walk confidently. Often it was necessary to hack down branches for firewood. Sometimes they found themselves caught in a thicket and had to cut their way through.

Frequently there were disagreements about the route. The Old Catholic was confident that God would direct them and sometimes insisted that his inspiration about the correct path should be trusted because God was actually leading them. The *converso*, piqued by the Old Catholic's solid religious credentials, sometimes suspected that the man of devotion was lording it over him and taking advantage of his lower status in the Christian community to assert his will. At such times, the repentant sinner had to intervene and it was most often his vote that decided the direction. Generally he trusted the *converso*'s compass and could yet assure the Old Catholic that his reliance on the North Star was also correct and reliable.

11

It was clear to all of them, naturally, that to split up would be disadvantageous and dangerous to each one, so they hung together in spite of disagreements. Though each of them had a different motive and purpose for making the pilgrimage, the most fundamental fact was their need for each other. The risks of going it alone seemed less desirable than the often considerable inconvenience and irritation of going together.

It was almost unthinkable to consider making a pilgrimage alone, though it had been known that some rather eccentric sorts had done so. But these three men all had something to come home to—a business, a family, a future. They preferred the possibility of returning to the future together rather than the possibility of making a name for themselves as heroic and individualistic achievers of the nearly impossible.

The text of the story I received does not give an ending. Surely, they sometimes had to stop. They had no control over time. Darkness would fall, and they would have to stop. Rains would pour, and they would have to take shelter. Disagreements and old resentments would sometimes erupt with such intensity that they could not continue, and the political realities, if you will, would prove as intransigent as the end of day and beginning of night.

The most likely ending is probably this: They were on a pilgrimage together to catch up with the larger group ahead of them. They trusted the one with the experience. They were inspired by the man of devotion. They relied on the repentant man to resolve their worst differences. They used their sticks to make their way. They shared the work of the journey and survival together. They had a goal bigger than reconciling their diversity or their disagreements. It was a sacred place they wanted to get to as individuals, but they needed the others to get there.

Did they reach the Holy Land? Did they return to their native place? I suppose we only discover the ending by setting out on the same pilgrimage.

The Mission of the Unpartnered Woman and the Gospel for Today

Introduction

Jesus said to the woman, "God call your husband, and come back." The woman answered and said to him, "I do not have a husband." Jesus answered her, "You are right in saying 'I do not have a husband.' For you have had five husbands, and the one you now have is not your husband. What you have said is true." The woman said to him, "Sir, I can see that you are a prophet."... The woman... went into the town and said to the people, "Come see a man who told me everything I have done." (NAB John 4:16–18, 29)

A few weeks ago, I began teaching a course on the Gospel of John to thirty-five seminary students. I have taught this material many times. In spite of the familiarity of the story of the woman at the well in the fourth chapter of John, I have never found students to be bored with the dialogue between Jesus and the Samaritan woman. She seems to exercise an eternal appeal, as though she were a sort of Marilyn Monroe of the first century. As an opener to the discussion, I asked the students how they have heard this story taught and preached. What are the theological themes associated with the Samaritan woman's story? The first answer was "forgiveness." Then followed "conversion," "mission," "apostleship," "living water," "messiahship of Jesus, " "belief," and "baptism."

After affirming the better answers, I returned to the first claim of the story's theme, forgiveness. "What makes this a forgiveness story? Is this woman a sinner? What is her sin?" The usual answers were given. "She came out to get water at noon, so this proves she had a bad reputation and was ashamed to show her face with the women who came to draw water in the morning. Her sin was her reckless lifestyle. She had five husbands, wasn't married, and was living with another man." But, I said, there is no word for sin, or an act of forgiveness in the entire story. Jesus never says, "Go and sin no more," or "Your sins are forgiven you." He certainly does take up the matter of sinning with the man paralyzed for thirty-eight years, "See, you are well. Sin no more, that nothing worse befall you" (John 5:14).

And he minces no words with the adulteress, "I do not condemn you. God and do not sin again" (John 8:11) . If the evangelist wants to talk about sin and forgiveness, he does.

We are left with the problem: How can the Samaritan woman's story be about a sinful woman and her forgiveness if nothing is said about sin or forgiveness? We know the possible consequences for women of this interpretation. Even if a woman goes out on mission, it's with the memory of her sinfulness and God's act of forgiveness.

Jesus is always the one who forgives. Other people only believe the woman when she reminds them of her life-long history of sinning. Maybe they come to Jesus, the man who told her everything she ever did because they want to hear all the details of all her sins? Is the effectiveness of the woman as the first missionary intrinsically tied to her repentance as a converted sinner?

Our assumptions about the Samaritan woman, and our conditioned interpretation about her story present some of the issues I would like to address. Why does John choose this woman as a prototype of the mission of the entire Church? What is her reality as a woman that makes her a model for both men and women as followers of Jesus? Is it because she is a sinful woman to start with, or because we are to confront the paradox of what she seems to be as a woman versus what she actually is as the first missionary in John's gospel. What she seems to be to us is not the woman Jesus sees her to be. Christ's vision of this particular woman's truth is healing and freeing, both for the woman and for all the people of her city.

I would like to engage the perspective that John the evangelist does: the Samaritan woman embodies what it means to be an unpartnered woman, what it means to be a conscious woman, and what it means to be a woman with a mission. I would like to propose the Samaritan woman as the model for celibate women whose mission in the Church today is still good news. The Samaritan woman incarnates the best human energies of the Church. She is the image of what the Church still needs today if the Church is to be faithful to giving people living water for their real thirsts, not stagnant water for their imagined needs.

To advance this reflection, I will deal with three themes we connect with celibacy: witness, end-time and mission. I'd like to review some theological aspects of our own training in the meaning of celibacy and its articulation in the past. Then I would like to acknowledge what I believe has broken down in that theology and why some aspects of the older theology seem to have lost their force. Finally, I would like to set out some directions for a new articulation of what celibacy can mean for us as women. Celibacy is a kind of code for all the power we have to love one another, to serve those in need of healing, and to commit ourselves to the slow work of nurturing an ailing Church, specifically as women.

I. The Past Articulation of Celibacy

1. Witness

We remember that the roots of our religious commitment go back to the first century. During times of persecution, many Christians gave up their lives because of acknowledging Jesus. Baptism and membership in the Christian community involved a life-threatening choice; being baptized meant sometimes quite literally being baptized into the death of Jesus. These were the martyrs. Martyr comes from the Greek word for witness. The martyr or witness was a man or woman who proclaimed the gospel by dying for it.

Witness also meant, by extension, preaching the gospel as though your life depended on it. Preaching and teaching required making a public show of your faith and having everyone know who you were. This made you a witness, too, because of the risk to your life, and the fact that prior to your death, you could very well end up on trial before judges and condemned by law to die. "They will hand you over for judgment before governors and kings" (Luke 21:12). The first martyrs, witnesses, and preachers took as their example the role of the suffering Jesus. Just as Jesus had been accused of wrong-doing, brought to trial, and condemned to death, so would the witness of Jesus. The first martyrs, preachers, and pastors of the Church, witnessing to the gospel, laid down their lives as a consequence of everyone knowing who they were.

2. End-Time

When the decades of persecution ceased, and baptism into the faith no longer entailed a threat of death, what did total commitment of oneself to Jesus involve? How should witness be given? When the enemy isn't there, Christians sought other ways to live heroically. This was also an issue early in the Gospels during the second generation of the Church. When the coming of Jesus seemed delayed, how should one live? The Gospels and Pastoral Epistles deal with this question of settling down for the long wait until Jesus would return. The end-time became ordinary time. We find this awareness in the New Testament when pastors give advice to their congregations about the way husbands should relate to their wives—love them and care for them as Christ loved the Church (Eph 5:21–33), how communities are to choose leaders (I Timothy 3), and what forgiveness Christians are to extend to one another (Luke 15:3–42), how they are to console one another when they face the death of their loved ones (I Thess 4:13–18).

But there were many who sought a more radical context than family life in "ordinary time" for being faithful to the gospel. The new heroism required a life-long state of martyrdom, standing at the threshold between this life and the life to come. An ideal of death to the world inspired many Christians to leave the cities and retreat to the desert. In the desert, devout Christians could live at the edge of life, with their whole attention on the reality of resurrection and the life to come. Witness in the desert was a lifestyle that rejected the complexity and corruption of the city at a time when social structures were breaking down. Witness was an embodied refusal to be a part of what was passing away, and a protest against what was destructive to a conception of the highest possibilities for achieving full humanity.

When Christians with this mindset faced the end of the world, they didn't worry about the future, about having children to carry on their name, about taking care of property, about playing the game to get ahead in society or keep their jobs. Political power and obedience to its demands ceased to be a concern, since all the world's institutions were temporary. The real social order was imagined as a new reality. The kingdom of God was a concept that described the experience of a new order to be disclosed after resurrection, beyond death, and waiting for Jesus to return meant keeping one's whole attention on him. At the same time, no one knew when Jesus would return.

Waiting for the end-time in this intense expectation of change became ordinary time.

Something of the meaning of the vows has its origin in this impulse to go out to the desert. The new martyrdom was lived out by living radically the letting go of a claim on property, and letting go of plans to have power and control. This expressed the conviction that the world's institutions and political structures were passing away. Man men and women went out to the desert. They were inspired not by a law requiring them to observe celibacy, but by an urgency to live in terms of a future life. Christians did not invent celibate commitment as the expression of their dedication. Several generations of Jewish inhabitants of the monastery at Qumran, near the Dead Sea, also lived a celibate life. The desert holds the secret of much of our strength as celibate women. Much of what continually has inspired women religious can be recovered by a remembrance of our historical precedents. Providing a rationale today for women's celibate commitment still can be found in a retrieval of why dedication to Jesus among the early generations of Christians took the form of life in the desert.

As apostolic religious life evolved, its external expressions changed. We can trace the development by where people lived and what they did during the day. Earliest religious life was lived by hermits, then by hermits living near each other and coming together occasionally. This was the cenobitic style. Then was the monastic expression in which many persons lived under one roof. Then came the mendicant preachers who took to the streets. Instead of the work coming to them, they went to the work. The apostolic communities looked at the challenge of the explorations of the new world as field for missionary enterprise. A new generation of religious communities meeting social needs arose beginning in the last three centuries. The schools, hospitals, orphanages, and other institutions of compassionate care all entailed a challenge to civil government for its neglect of so many in need.

3. Mission

We can look at the evolution of religious life not only in terms of external changes of lifestyle, but through the lens of a changing sense of mission. The mission of those who fled the city to go to the desert was a personal commitment to the gospel, an urgency to model one's whole life on those moments in the life of Jesus that expressed his radical commitment to God. The desert fathers and mothers left us a record of their sayings and spiritual counsel. And much of it is focused on spiritual wholeness, starting life over while becoming reconciled with one's past, reclaiming the dark side of the self, finding an inner balance and peace, and reorienting one's whole energies to God.

As the desert population of witnesses grew, mission became expressed in forming community with large numbers of people. We know the evolution in service that took place in Benedictine monastic community life—liturgical praise, education for those who came to the monastery, agrarian cooperatives. During the dark centuries in the West, it was the monasteries that preserved the records of culture and learning. It was the monastery that presented some semblance of orderly society when political leaders could no longer preserve order. The monastery was a city unto itself and embodied what it meant to be a Church of prayer, common worship, a community of loving support, and a place to offer service to the world. There remains much about us that bears the best of these centuries of monastic life.

The mission of mendicant orders of the late middle ages was expressed when they took to the streets, recognizing that the teaching and preaching that needed to be done could not be confined to the walls of the monastery. The monastery had been the place where people came to be served. The mendicants reversed that direction, left their monasteries. Often, the people they reached out to were Christians who felt alienated from the Church's traditional structure and doctrine.

The apostolic communities of the Reformation took their cue from the exploration of the globe and the discovery by Europeans of new lands across the ocean. Missionary communities sought to carry the gospel message to the peoples of far-off lands, to take European culture to them, and to advance the Church's mission to the ends of the earth. They developed a spirituality for the road, and an understanding of community and prayer that put both at the service of the worldwide missionary enterprise.

At the same time, reform movements within the monastic communities called them back to the early ideals of stability and centeredness, with the heart concentrated on the one thing necessary, union with God.

Then, in the last three centuries, in the rise of the industrial revolution and the urbanization of European culture, it was evident that the needs of many people had been overlooked. New communities of compassion arose to respond to the educational, health care, and advocacy needs of those groups that fell between the cracks. These communities bear the evolutionary history of all that preceded them. And today, these communities, visible within institutions as they are, show the Church quite clearly that it is in the midst of radical change.

4. Reflection on End-Time

Like my students, who assumed there must be something wrong with the Samaritan woman, we may have internalized the suspicion that there is something wrong with women's religious life. We are told that we would not be suffering a decline in numbers if we were giving better witness to the gospel, if people could see us for what are in the right clothes, if we lived more simply, if we were more obedient, less determined to have participative forms of government, less feminist and more authentic, prayerful, and responsive to the Holy Spirit.

I think this tendency needs to be resisted as well as the impulse to accept the blame others assign us and then blame ourselves. I do not believe we are at fault. There are so many changes in the Church and society that we give witness to, that we should ask a different, life-giving question: How are we witnesses to the end-time of this period in the Church? What is the truth our experience offers the Church, and what directions does that suggest she take for her future? In other words, I believe we live a richly prophetic moment for the entire Church. What is truly happening to her shows in us. If she wants to read her own possibilities, and see how the Spirit is truly acting, she can continue to look to women who have faithfully been living religious life. She can see the changes they have made, not as deviance from religious ideals, but as hope for the entire Church. Like the Samaritan woman, a religious women's community is more than it seems. In spite of appearances, it is an especially gifted and appropriate responder to the mission of the Jesus. Jesus likes the Samaritan woman. Even though she is alone and seems socially problematic, she has the gifts needed for carrying out the mission. She is the one who is the paradigm for what discipleship is.

II. What Has Broken Down in the Older Articulation of Witness, End-Time, and Mission

It has only been the last twenty years or so that we really knew we were in the middle of deep change. Like a windmill with its blades responding to the breeze, religious communities of women have felt the movements that come rushing at them unseen, but felt. We have been faithfully transmitting the energy of the truth of social change to the Church. We have been women who tell the truth to the Church. One thing we say is that the theological language by which the Church has described us needs to be shaken out and given another look. The language for our motivation and ideals, our lifestyle and mission doesn't match our changing experience of commitment to Jesus and the Church.

1. The Concept of Witness is Undergoing Change

One change we are all aware of is that the last twenty-five years have generated a "democratization of holiness." Holiness as a call to close union with God is everyone's claim as a baptized person. The Pastoral Constitution on the Church in the Modern World broke down a hierarchical notion of holiness, with some more holy than others because of lifestyle. The dignity of motherhood, marriage and doing the work of social justice has been affirmed in many Church documents. And this is a good and Spirit-inspired direction.

A second change has to do with the connection we experience between our lifestyle and the person—interior work we have undertaken to become healed and whole as individuals. In relation to the healing of life's hurts, the language of the vows, our cycle of hours of prayer, community activities, our entire horarium of prayer, community, and work shows signs of being in transition.

What inspired our prayer, and described our relationship with God today seems to want a new language. Having been deeply faithful to our horarium, we know that these practices in themselves have not brought about healing of life's painful experiences. Women have important personal needs and questions that the traditional lifestyle cannot always provide an answer for, nor the sacrament of confession, nor spiritual direction alone.

Another kind of conversation is needed to bring about inner healing. Support groups spring up, and we take advantage of counseling. There seems an urgency to attend to healing, face our addictions, work toward spiritual, emotional and intellectual integration. The Holy Spirit seems to be calling us to live at a deeper level. And this impulse for healing that takes us beyond the limits of healing that we used to experience in living religious life is a good direction for individuals and the community. Jesus healed people deeply and totally. Likewise, it is gospel wholeness and transformation we seek as we make use of all the means available: individual counseling, support groups and theological reflection groups. From any quarter we can find it, we seek strength to transcend life's many hurts especially those we experience and suffer because we share the lot of women culturally and historically.

A third change has to do with our expectations of community. We have lived community, but there are many aspects about ourselves in relationship that don't get addressed in the theology of community life. We want something deeper than what we have experienced with one another thus far and we want closer bonds of understanding. We are amazed sometimes that we could have lived in the same congregation so long and know our Sisters less well than we would like.

I think an impulse toward finding inner wholeness is very strong today, and an impulse toward a deeper quality of communication, though our psychological categories for describing these have changed from the days of the desert dwellers. Thus, there is today a return to some essential aspects of the desert period of religious life, its eremetical and cenobitic expressions that allowed for healing and deepening to take place in a conversation with a master. In the desert, one could concentrate on the relationships that were most essential for maintaining communion with God, experiencing support in the quest for wholeness and integration.

Even while we give ourselves to our institutional mission, the need to retreat from the "city" of institutional and community life reflects some deep spiritual and historical impulses. At the same time, we find that fifteen hundred years of evolution in religious life leaves us many tensions as we seek to be faithful to the mission we have not only to others but to ourselves. Living in the end-time means we are faithful to the reality that no one can live our life for us. But we find that we must live more questions than answers today. Like the Samaritan woman, we give ourselves to the conversation with Jesus, without knowing what will be the result. We stay there in the dialogue, responding, questioning, debating, and telling the truth, like the Samaritan woman.

We don't know what Jesus is going to do with all that because we are in the middle of talking and responding to him. But the Church gives us a story about what happens as a result of that conversation, and this is affirmation for us, even in the middle of our theological debate. The woman said, "Our ancestors worshipped here in this place, but you Judeans have called us heretics and said Jerusalem is the place where we ought to worship. What do you have say about that issue?" (John 4:20) Jesus gives her an unexpected answer, and gives her an unexpected mission.

A fourth change that affects the understanding of our witness as celibate religious women is related to a new respect for the body. We see daily that more people are exercising and watching their diet than ever before, and this is a general social trend. There is a movement to see the body as a blessing rather than a focus for discipline and self-denial. In society, there is a greater reverence for the body and attention to its communication. We see a rejection of an older Manichean ideal of the body as evil. We are much more sophisticated in our thinking about sexuality than decades ago. We hear a more enlightened theology of marriage, which places the loving relationship of spouses at the center of their commitment, displacing the duty of procreation as the primary purpose of marriage.

Marriage is for love, and from love come children. Sexuality as the description of gender roles is also being rethought in feminist inquiry, gay-lesbian discourse, concerns over the technologies of reproduction, and the abortion debate. But changed attitudes toward the body also affect our thinking about the reason we chose a lifestyle other than marriage.

More knowledge and enlightenment about our life-giving energy and our sexuality betoken a wonderful social change. To love and respect the body that God gave us, to understand its rhythms and needs, is something of relief, yet it also raises complex questions for celibates. We sense the problematic represented by the changed attitude toward sexuality and embodiment. We have to rethink celibacy in relation to sexuality As a result, many people have felt permission to trust their sexual desires. They are free to choose what lifestyle they want. Is this freedom in the Church to be suppressed?

The result of knowledge, freedom and changed perception of sexuality seems, in part, to have affected religious life negatively. Not as many, it seems, really want to live a celibate commitment. But is the blessing on sexual communion that now exists in the Church to be taken away, because many more people know that marriage is a holy state of life? Shall celibates say there is something wrong with the way they live their commitment because more people who thirst for deep relationship with God feel free to get married now instead of remaining celibate? No, what is required is a deeper rethinking and explanation for the viability and integrity of what celibate witness means when corporality and sexuality are affirmed.

2. The Changing Meaning of End-Time

Facing the end of the world has been taken very seriously, perhaps more seriously by more people than ever before. But a very normal expression of facing the end of the world today has been to join the peace movement and work for the containment of the nuclear arms race. A Sister works on environmental issues. Another assists in projects for famine relief so people's lives will not end sooner than they should. We are growing more conscious of the reality of the end of the world, and how it is in our power to either forestall or bring that destruction about.

Thus, the older notion that the end of the world will be visited upon us by God is being revised. That idea that religious witness means living in terms of the life to come is diluted by the urgency to prevent the end of the world by nuclear holocaust or environmental disaster. Facing the end of the world does not compel a person necessarily to enter a religious community, nor does it clearly mandate a radical leave-taking of "the world" in the form of religious life. The point is to stave off the end of the world and the death of the planet. This requires massive numbers of people engaged in peace-making and peace-keeping. It requires engagement of the world, not departure from it. Should we be unhappy that the end of the world has become a reality to so many more people than celibate religious? Aren't we relieved that thousands and millions of people worldwide are concerned about the end of the world and have done something about it out of love and concern for the world community?

Liberation theology is another movement related to end-time that has affected thinking about religious life. Liberation theology challenges and disagrees with the notion that people should live with their eyes fixed on the next life, and bear their sufferings of the present time with fortitude and patience. That whole spirituality has been thrown out the window. Why? It perpetuates injustice to the poor, the uneducated and the propertyless to expect them to pray in earthly misery while expecting heaven, while the rich live comfortably during this life.

Those engaged in social justice act from a conviction that God intends to bring about justice here on earth. Suffering and endurance in light of a future reward is a spiritual vision that benefits the rich, not the poor. Instead of an end-time theology that sees the reality as heaven or a world "up there," the emphasis is on assisting the emergence of a new social order here below. We know that this changed vision of end-time is a new form of witness, for it antagonizes people in power and results in death for those who work for justice to the poor.

It may be a problem for religious communities that the older eschatological spirituality has lost its appeal. But would any of us say that the poor should lack education, property and sustenance right now? Would any of us say that they should continue to suffer because they will get a reward in heaven? Our good sense and compassion say this change reflects the mission of Jesus, even though the consequences end up making our own future contingent. In this, we share the lot of the poor—a contingent future, an uncertain tomorrow. Is this condition alien to the spirit and values of radical religious commitment from its beginning in the desert?

3. A Changing Understanding of Charism and Mission

We have understood mission as the desire to work with each other, but we now see one another engaged in individual tasks. How is this corporate mission? I believe this tension has resulted from being faithful to the Church's call that we reexamine our original charism. It may have been the expectation that once we revived a sense of our original charism, we would all put our shoulders to the wheel of the common tasks with more energy, and push together with renewed vigor and vision. But just the opposite seems to have happened. There is now greater diversity in our ministerial life than ever before. And we cannot fault our Sisters' impulses to attend to those in direct need who have no one else to take care of them. We find that we need to do what comes from our compassion at another's misery. Obedience to this inner conviction was at the root of the foundation of our congregations of apostolic service. We find this charismatic fidelity in tension with corporate commitments our communities have made. A return to our roots has made us redefine what we mean by corporate sponsorship of institutions. The founding moment each of us must live as a member of the congregation has seemed for the moment to generate diversity rather than uniformity. Have we gained or lost?

The impulse of religious life is there, but it often turns its attention to the people who fall between the cracks—the very sorts of persons who evoked the creation of new religious families of service in the first place. But the recovery of this original impulse for mission seems to be pulling us apart rather than summoning up our collective energy. How are we to evaluate the changes in the way we are carrying out our corporate mission? Is it a good thing that we act from genuine compassion as individuals? Is it a good thing that someone takes care of the people who fall between the cracks? Even though we feel our numbers spread thinner and thinner, is it against the gospel to follow the impulse itself to do what our heart inspires us? Surely we affirm one another's compassion, even as we feel its cost to us communally.

In addition to the individual and corporate expression of our mission, another change we acknowledge has to do with the theological starting place for explaining our service. A theology of ministry has shifted its base from priestly to baptismal, and from sacramental to charismatic, or the interiorly inspired. A new emphasis is given to the unique giftedness or charism of each person. There is a shift from ministry defined as the official function of the sacramentally ordained, to an understanding of ministry as connected with people's native talents bestowed on them as gifts to be used for the entire Church. Respect for giftedness of all persons has drawn emphasis away from specialized, celibate people entrusted to carry on the Church's ministry.

There is an obvious shift to practical dependence on the participation of married women and men in parishes, schools, and church-sponsored social services, health care, care of the elderly, and advocacy for special needs, from AIDS to latch-key children. Is this shift in ministerial theology, with greater participation on the work of all the people of God, to be faulted? Surely we say again that religious women know and support these changes, even as a changed theology impacts our numbers. We know that it not necessary to be a celibate, unpartnered woman to take care of people within the Church and attend to their spiritual needs, because laity also are full participants in the ministries.

Are we not to rejoice that so many hands join ours now than ever before? We know as well as anyone, that people will never stop being sick, cease from dying, or need to be comforted and visited. People will never stop needing a prayerful setting for worship, the strength of a sacramental encounter with Jesus, access to spiritual nourishment and the support of a believing community. Are we not to rejoice in the fact that so many more people have this awareness and are ready to do something about it, even though they do not live under our roof?

Changes in our actual experience of mission have impacted the way we understand living the vows. A certain spectrum of virtues used to be "evidence" that we were "fulfilling" our vows, such as fidelity to ordinary, daily tasks, which were often hidden from public view. Another virtue was cooperative and willing submission to authority. The ways to be a "good nun" and a virtuous woman, however, were often in tension with the massiveness of the tasks we faced within our institutions and our advocacy roles. In our institutions, for example, exercise of virtue called for more assertive conduct, such as forthrightness, decisiveness, and active intervention. Virtues that used to measure our holiness within community, such as patience, humility, and unending tolerance, didn't always match the demands of our ministries.

We suspect that many of the virtues prescribed for women religious came from men's recipe for what an ideal wife in a patriarchal household should be like. We remember that most of the spiritual reading from the last seventy-five years on our library shelves was written by men. "Heritage of Violence," the Canadian bishops' document about women's concerns (Fall, 1989) admits responsibility the Church takes for proposing to women a set of religious values that feed the cycle of domestic violence. The questioning of what constitutes the holiness of women has been done by feminists who are committed women of faith. More and more men, too, note the injustice to women in the Church. The socialization of women into second-class citizenship within the Church in the name of tradition or "virtue" is increasingly a cause of concern. Should we be unhappy that our spirituality is being reexamined in light of our relationship with all women? What freedom lies in store for us and what renewal of strength. Wouldn't we be happy to know there is less violence against women because women have begun to take hold of their strengths and redefine what a virtuous woman really is?

4. Reflection

Religious life is still a witness, but it is a witness and a testimony to the deep changes taking place in society. What we experience as breakdown and loss is actually evidence of great creative change for the better in the Church at large. The Samaritan woman's life may seem to be a problem at first reading, because our expectations demand that she should be conducting her relationships according to a certain norm of social propriety. But a second reading makes us confront a paradox. An unpartnered woman with a history of five husbands, and still counting, is seen by the evangelist as an especially capable woman for carrying out the mission of Jesus. Everything about her seems to be wrong, but she's the right person as far as Jesus is concerned. Why? Because she responds to change, because she knows what is going on in the world around her, because she is in touch with the right theological questions, because she debates the questions, because she is not afraid, because she reflects, and because she knows how to talk to a whole city of people and get them to listen to her. "Come and see the man who told me everything I ever did."

III. Directions for a New Articulation of Celibacy

1. Celibacy as Witness

I think we could recover a sense of celibacy not as sexual abstinence, but as spiritual and social autonomy. Our unmarried state, freely chosen, allows us the possibility of many social roles. As women, we make a proclamation that our lives have integrity and worth in themselves, apart from dependence on any social or economic role in relation to a man. A woman is whole. Her life is worth having been lived, without a before and without an after, without husband, without children, without in-laws, without a household, without someone's name and without partnership with a man.

This is a deep implication of what freedom of celibacy means. Radical feminism of the twentieth century did not invent convictions about the worth of women. The Church has always had a hard-line core of feminists, celibate women who embody the Church's abiding tradition of radical feminism and its potential commitment to the cause of all women. There remains a need for radical feminism at the heart of the Church. Celibate women make incarnate that possibility for seeing women in a light other than a domestic one. A woman has personal integrity and future that are both independent of her subjection to a man's authority within the household.

It takes energy and insight to live as a celibate women. Celibacy can only be sustained by women who have a deep wisdom, radical understanding of what it means to be human, full responsibility for themselves, and internal resources for sustaining a life of great risk. Women are not supposed to be free and autonomous. They are supposed to find their meaning in relation to a male partner. They are supposed to have a man to obey in a man's world. Celibate women are the Church's traditional feminists who have always lived a challenge to this definition of woman and men's theologizing which makes her traditional role God's will. I think the sisterhood we live is desperately needed as a source of hope to all women.

The Samaritan woman, Jesus said, probably with some humor, had had five husbands and the man who accompanied her presently was not her husband. Ironically, this means she was a woman undefined by domestic partnership and marriage. No children are mentioned. Jesus doesn't say, "Go call your husband and children." So she's either post-menopausal with grown children, or else she doesn't have children at all. Jesus calls her "Woman," a title that addresses her as she is in herself, not wife-of-a-man, or mother-of-little-children. Jesus gets down to the core of who she is, a person who is autonomous, undefined by any husband or any man at all. And she is the one who is given the mission that stands for the mission of the entire Church. She is a witness to Jesus first of all because she is an autonomous woman.

A second aspect of celibacy as witness that calls for new articulation is the social meaning of celibacy. Our sisterhood as unpartnered women potentially touches and embraces all women, especially the unpartnered. We have sisterly bonds with the divorced and separated, lesbians, widows, battered women, the sexually abused, prostitutes, the disabled, and single mothers living in poverty. We share the same unpartnered state as the teenager longing for the ideal mate and the woman waiting for her spouse to return from the war. Any woman who has no partner is our sister.

We see that we all share a common life task: to find meaning in our long or short-term solitude, to become healed and whole, to find new strength to live our own lives, and to give ourselves in loving relationships. We trust the deep wisdom of women abut sexuality and friendship. The number of women who leave their marriages is a public witness to the Church and society that being unpartnered, without a sexual relationship, is preferable to an abusive relationship, or a marriage in which there is no love. Women accept poverty, the burden of caring for their children, all manner of social and economic restrictions, public embarrassment and loss of status, as well as a Church that marginalizes them. All this they confront and choose instead of a marriage that requires that they accept emotional or physical abuse. I think women have a vision of relationship that is trustworthy. Women, finally, do not define themselves sexually, but as persons who demand respect and love as the basis of any expression relationship takes, be it sexual or not. I suppose Jesus recognized that the Samaritan woman had this vision of relationship. "I have no husband." And He chose this woman as a missionary. I think we can trust that wisdom about what is really important in relationships between men and women resides in us and our sisters.

A third aspect of celibacy as witness can be understood as a taking hold of my own story, my life themes and explaining how the history through which I have lived has impacted my spirit and shaped my understanding of God. I think celibate witness means we are called to have a prophetic vision of our own lives, as we look back, and see our lives in terms of the blessing we have lived. Undertaking the challenging work of self-healing is a primary way we are faithful to our call as unpartnered women. "Come see the man who told me everything I ever did," may have little to do with the woman's sexual history, but much to do with the grasp Jesus had of her entire life story. Something in the conversation with Jesus gave her a true picture of her history, and this retelling of her life gave her joy, not shame. "All that she ever did" is a celebration, not a confession of sin. "All that she ever did" is a way to describe a sense of her full power and possibility, present from the beginning.

Instinctively, among close friends, in support groups and theological reflections groups, we are making public our story, sometimes of recovery, sometimes of struggle, sometimes of searching. But it is our story, not someone else's. It is our personal witness to healing and wholeness, to the truth of our changes and to our expanding vision. The involvement of more persons in training for spiritual direction reflects this instinct that our own "story of the soul" is God's power acting through us. Celibacy as witness to the autonomy of women requires that the story of a woman's wholeness be told. I think there is strength for the people of God in this valuing of our own personal history, and the deepened sense of God acting in the plotline of our life. I suppose this is the way women have always enacted Eucharist, and always will, ordained or not. They will always hand over to one another a life-giving story about themselves.

2. Rethinking Celibacy and the Relationship to End-Time

We are looking at an ending of our period of strength in numbers and this form of security for the future. "We will be in the next decades fewer, older, and poorer," said a member of our council. It is a unique end-time for us. Yet we say like the martyrs before us, "This commitment is worth my life. I am glad that I chose to stay with these women whom I love as we faced the end together." And we don't know what kind of end-time it is. We feel the vulnerability of uncertainty about our future. Like the martyrs Perpetua and Felicity, we go arm and arm into the Coliseum to face the lions and tigers. We live at the edge of death in courage and confidence. We don't know if our community as a whole will be spared or taken. Will we find our present life taken away and transformed with God in eternity? Or will the life of our community continue in some renewed way? Like the martyrs who belonged to a contingent and fragile Christian community, persecuted from all sides, we are ready for the translation of ourselves and our lives into the future that belongs to God.

This is one meaning of Eucharist. Jesus gives up his physical way of being present in the world. He had the power to go on living, yet he gave up bodily presence in space and time. He exchanged one kind of presence for another, that of being in the world through bread and wine. He chose to continue his life through a community of love, memory, and replication of his actions. To participate in the Eucharist as women may not presently mean saying the words of consecration over bread and wine. But we know certainly that we are celebrating the Eucharist when we live in willingness that our lives and our work be handed over to a future we do not control. We celebrate Eucharist when our power to serve is given over into the hands of others who are willing to lay down their lives with the same hope and conviction we have had. Celibate women give a witness to the meaning of Eucharist that is distinct from the understanding men have.

In line with women's understanding of Eucharist, we can consider "institutional celibacy" as those attitudes that we communicate through sponsorship. We are willing to let go of the certainty that other bodies will come from this community, that there will be our own children, as it were, heading the family business. We are willing to embrace new kinds of shared ministry and continuation of service as we let go of control. Not perpetuating ourselves physically or institutionally, we are willing to let go of the certainty that our life will continue in space and time in exactly the same way. We let ourselves in our institutions become Eucharist. This is a profound handing over of our lives and entrusting of all we are to God as we give up our multigenerational leases on a future that is certain.

Just as witness is given when we tell our own story, end-time living involves a corporate and prophetic remembering of past history as we claim its strength. End-time means we name what is ending and we try to describe what is beginning. We acknowledge the ending, and give our energy to beginning. We trust our experience, our good sense and our vision of reality. As celibate women, we don't have to make up stories to protect our husbands or our children from painful truths. We have a greater freedom to live without illusion, because we have so little to protect. We can see that all movements in religious life resulted from a breakdown or inadequacy in what came before. We would not have the story of the Samaritan women in John's gospel if the community had thought Mark's gospel was the last word to be said about Jesus. What is true about Scripture is true about us as women religious.

3. Rethinking our Understanding of Celibacy and Mission

We can see the sponsorship of our large institutions as the equivalent for women of episcopal leadership of a diocese. What a bishop should do for a diocese, that is what we do for our institutions. As episcopal leaders, we take responsibility within institutions for bringing about the participation of laity and other women in the work of the Church. What religious women are doing in their own institutions is what the entire Church should do. Celibate women's style of sponsorship is the graced alternative to patriarchal and authoritarian control within the Church. What the Church should be, women's institutions already embody. We should not overlook our prophetic activity on behalf of our coworkers. The values we operate from within our institutions are what the Church needs to generate its own ecclesial renewal. The mission of celibate women requires imagining the future of the Church in a new way. From the experience of sharing power with men in models of participative management, religious women restructure styles of authority that are available through example to the Church.

A young priest came to me for advice. We talked about his relationships with women. He said he valued his priestly commitment to the Church and was determined to be careful about his relationships with women. I said something along these lines: "Do you know what people do when they are afraid of someone else? The create distance to gain safety, or they assemble massive weapons of defense, or else they try and dominate the other by weakening or destroying the person they are afraid of . . . Most of the people you will minister to in the Church will be women. Most of your coworkers will be women. Maybe you want to think of some other response than being careful of women."

I generally have counseled seminarians that a priest should be a man of justice, strategic planning, invitation, and a persona capable of orchestrating the gifts of others. And he had better love women very much and feel comfortable with them or else shouldn't be a priest.

We can trust that how women live celibacy holds the secret of the Church's mission. We chose to live not from the position of greater clerical power, but from radical love, with little ecclesial or social advantage. "Come and see a man who told me all that I ever did." It is my history of loving and not giving up. My history of trying to be fruitful and make my life with others work out. It's my struggle with the theological questions of my day. It's my willingness to cross the boundaries of traditional prejudices, like the old norms that separated Jewish men from Samaritan women. It's my determination to live in terms of a conversation, not a set of prohibitions about my behavior. It's all the courage I have to go on loving in spite of failed relationships, in spite of unrequited love, and in spite of a future that I hoped for that didn't turn out. Finally, everything I ever did, and everything I suffered, along with all my loving—this becomes the energy Jesus can engage for mission.

The Samaritan woman stands for all celibate, unpartnered women entrusted with the Church's mission. And what unpartnered women do for the Church is what the Church should for the entire community of believers. "Come and see the man who told me everything I ever did."

Initiatives for the Burlingame Chapter

Governance Directions

Within the regional community the regional president . . . exercises personal authority according to Church law, the Institute Constitutions and the regional community government plan. (Constitutions § 74)

1. The RLT shall exercise leadership in acknowledgment of the threefold reality that Sisters have status
    - as baptized faithful of the Church
    - as members of a religious community with vows
    - as U.S. citizens.

2. The RLT shall govern in light of their threefold responsibilities:
    - as those who exercise legitimate authority within the Institute
    - as leaders who uphold gospel values and Church teaching
    - as officers of the religious corporation.

3. The RLT shall assiduously review the 1991 Constitutions and
    - explicitly lead the community according to this ecclesial document
    - seek in good faith to reform habits of governance rooted in prior constitutions and entitlements of the pre-Vatican II era
    - support a culture of participative governance and decision-making
    - be accountable for carrying out the regional government plan.

Due Process for Members

4.   In all relationships with members, leadership shall reverence the mystery of each Sister's consecration and commitment to God. Grateful for each member's vocation, leadership shall protect it as the Church's treasure and heritage. In accord with Constitutions § 77, regional leadership shall
   ➤ guarantee a canonical advocate to all Sisters in first and final profession
   ➤ not subject Sisters in first and final profession to dismissal proceedings or grieve them into leaving (constructive dismissal) without canonically-defined grounds
   ➤ not act apart from the norms of universal law as stated in Constitutions §49
   ➤ not act without strict adherence to ecclesial due process
   ➤ not act without a process of charity, equity, and respect as in Constitutions §50
   ➤ not act without formal Institute review according to Constitutions §67.

Non-observance of these provisions is grounds for removal from office. The process of removal from office is initiated by members though petition to the Institute President in accord with Constitutions §74: "Within the regional community the regional president [is] confirmed in office by the Institute president." "A chapter convoked by the first-elected councilor elects her successor." (Constitutions §63)

Educational Directions

5.   Educating itself for the performance of its responsibilities, the RLT will
   ➤ engage in on-going professional management counseling and coaching
   ➤ report its steps to undo the culture of parentalism in religious life
   ➤ counter a "mother-may-I" posture which casts members in the role of minor children
   ➤ listen to members with respect as adult contemporaries
   ➤ welcome the diversity of different viewpoints

6. The RLT shall manifest its commitment to the Institute Direction Statement regarding "equality of women in Church and society" by
   - supporting the educational initiative Opening Worlds of Mercy
   - incorporating readings from OWOM into its communications
   - quoting the theological voices of women in the Church and Institute
   - Collaborating in the priorities and work of the Institute Commission on Women in its focus on the human rights of women.

7. The RLT shall manifest its commitment to the Institute's theme of "Reverence the dignity of each person" by providing resources through which all members can be educated to the
   - Church's definition of the ecclesial rights of all the baptized in the 1983 Code
   - Church's teaching about the protection of rights of women with vows
   - exhortations about the dignity of persons in papal and episcopal teaching
   - ecclesial due process for all who work in Church-related institutions
   - the specific approach of women and Mercy charism to these themes.

8. The RLT and every Sister elected or appointed to leadership shall
   - acquaint herself with the Reconciliation Process
   - hold herself disposed to participate if a member requests conciliation or mediation at the regional level.
   - educate herself in skills for handling conflict through such means as training seminars in alternative dispute resolution.

9. The RLT shall manifest its commitment to develop and act from a multicultural, international perspective, and to end all forms of racism by

- giving voice to the experience of Hispanic, Black, Asian, and indigenous members of the Burlingame regional community and associates
- giving voice to members and associates who identify with any minority ethnicity and national heritage
- supporting initiatives that raise consciousness about the Church's traditional culture of anti-Semitism.

Publishing the Acts of Chapter and Burlingame Directory

10. The RLT shall promptly publish the Acts of the Chapter to all vowed members, and republish the Burlingame Directory as inserts for the Policy Handbook.

THE RECONCILIATION PROCESS
Revision of Procedure for Reconciliation

When any of you has a grievance against another, do you dare to take it to court before the unrighteous, instead of taking it before the saints? . . . Can it be that there is no one among you wise enough to decide between one believer and another . . . ? (I Cor 6:1, 5)

The regional communities maintain structures for the guarantee of the rights of all and for the exercise of authority with appropriate accountability between leaders and members (Constitutions § 77)

11. **Procedure When a Party Declines to Participate**
Existing Text
3. "Utilization of the reconciliation process requires that BOTH parties to the dispute agree to participate. Each person's decision in this regard is respected." (Introduction)

Revision
Utilization of the reconciliation process requires that both parties to the dispute agree to participate. If one party declines, the Reconciliation Board, at the request

of the party wishing to continue, proceeds to compile a report of the facts. The report can include narratives, summaries of interviews, statements by parties and witnesses, and relevant documents. The report is made available to the petitioner so that she can effectively proceed to the next regional community level, or to the Institute Level.

Revision of Subject Matter for Reconciliation Board

By our life in community and by sharing our faith and mission, we come to know ourselves as sisters and to form bonds of union and charity. Reverence for the unique gift of each member . . . helps us to live together in affection and mutual respect. (Constitutions § 18)

Community strengthens us for mission when we listen openly to one another, seek the common good and promote mutual trust. (Constitutions § 19)

12. **Inclusion of Membership Issues as Matter for Reconciliation**
Existing Text

"Exclusion: Matter which is NOT subject for referral to the Regional Community reconciliation process is understood to include:

Decisions related to membership involving the Sisters of perpetual profession for which canon law or particular law of the Institute make provision for recourse (e.g., imposed exclaustration, dismissal . . .)."

Revision

[Delete the exclusion of decisions related to membership]. Membership issues related to Sisters in first and final profession are reviewable. Leadership is accountable to the community for its strict adherence to canonical and Constitutional protections of members' rights.

Rationale: Any decision, *especially* if it is cast as a membership issue by leadership, and is a decision taken against the will of a Sister in first or final profession, justifies intervention by the Reconciliation

Board at the request of that aggrieved Sister. Any dispute can be represented as a "membership issue" and thus extinguish her ability to seek recourse through review by the Reconciliation Board

Creation of a Permanent Forum for Members to Participate in Governance

Each regional chapter is responsible for the adoption and amendment of its regional directory, subject to approval by the Institute president and council. (Constitutions § 55)

In virtue of membership each Sister assumes the responsibility to participate in the decision making processes of the Institute, regional and local communities. (Constitutions § 78)

13. Holding as sacrosanct as the opening prayer, the RLT shall guarantee a regular forum to members so they can present initiatives and proposals. Whatever the agenda, planners of each regional gathering and annual convocation shall invite members in advance to submit proposals/initiatives. If proposals are submitted, planning shall allow time for all vowed members to hear and discuss such initiatives face to face in large group. This process and discussion shall precede any vote, no matter what form the voting takes.

Consultation with Mercy Experts Required

Each regional chapter is responsible for the adoption and amendment of its regional directory, subject to approval by the Institute president and council. (Constitutions § 55)

In virtue of membership each Sister assumes the responsibility to participate in the decision making processes of the Institute, regional and local communities. (Constitutions § 78)

14. The RLT shall in good faith consult Mercy experts in the Institute on matters related to internal governance, e.g., the meaning of the vows, spiritual guidance of members, application of universal (canon) law to the regional community, and interpretation of the 1991 Constitutions and Directory. The RLT shall not make or enforce policies by consulting with

outside experts to the exclusion of its own member historians, theologians, scripture scholars, spiritual directors, psychologists, canonists, lawyers, archivists, experts in the Constitutions, writers about the charism of Catherine McAuley, and the like. Policies are normative only if reviewed and voted upon by membership according to the Constitutions.

Review of Existing Committees

Each regional chapter is responsible for the adoption and amendment of its regional directory, subject to approval by the Institute president and council. (Constitutions § 55)

In virtue of membership each Sister assumes the responsibility to participate in the decision making processes of the Institute, regional and local communities. (Constitutions § 78)

15. Within one year of installation, the RLT shall undertake a review of all existing committees and seek a general evaluation of their function and effectiveness from members at large. The evaluations will provide suggestions for revision, and shall be anonymous. The RLT shall appoint an ad hoc task force of members at large to review these evaluations. The task force will formulate initiatives and present them to the membership for discussion and approval.

Procedure for Changing Existing Policies in Handbook

Each regional chapter is responsible for the adoption and amendment of its regional directory, subject to approval by the Institute president and council. (Constitutions § 55)

In virtue of membership each Sister assumes the responsibility to participate in the decision making processes of the Institute, regional and local communities. (Constitutions § 78)

16. Norms for effecting changes to existing policies in the Handbook, or adding new ones shall follow this procedure:
    - The RLT, a committee, a committee representative or an individual Sister proposes the change to the community at large and a rationale in writing is provided.
    - The membership is provided adequate opportunity to review, discuss and question changes within small groups.
    - Feedback from the community on such proposals is summarized by a different group of members than the proposer of the changes.
    - The membership is provided adequate opportunity to review, question and discuss changes in the assembly.
    - The membership must affirm the change by a two-thirds vote taken at the annual Convocation or during Chapter for the change to become normative.

Participation in Decision Making about Finances

Each regional chapter is responsible for the adoption and amendment of its regional directory, subject to approval by the Institute president and council. (Constitutions § 55)

In virtue of membership each Sister assumes the responsibility to participate in the decision making processes of the Institute, regional and local communities. (Constitutions § 78)

17. A new board will be created. The Common Life and Finance Board is accountable to the membership at large. It shall serve as an ongoing structure that ensures participation of vowed members in financial decision making and accountability of leadership to members. The Board provides an ongoing structure for continuity of dialogue about:
    - practice of common life and interpretation of the vow of poverty
    - use of shared resources and the impact on members
    - education of members about finances
    - responsibilities for aging family members
    - acquisition of real estate and sale of any property

Review of Materials on Poverty, Wills, Cession, and Patrimony

Each regional chapter is responsible for the adoption and amendment of its regional directory, subject to approval by the Institute president and council. (Constitutions § 55)

Each regional community through its chapter delineates the following in its regional directory: the regional community governance structure and ways of amending it . . . (Constitutions §71)

The regional community chapter has policy-making authority subject to the Institute Constitutions, the acts of the Institute chapter and the policies of the Institute (Constitutions § 72)

18. The RLT shall appoint a task force of Burlingame Mercies to review materials given to the community on wills, cessions, and patrimony. Such materials include inserts in the Policy Handbook, and the Institute video-conference on Patrimony of May 30, 2002. The review shall consider correspondence with California civil law, with provisions of canon law, with the history of Catherine McAuley, the charism of the Institute, and the practical lived experience of members. The task force shall make an initial report at the next Convocation.

Respecting the Rights of Members
Budget for Canonical Counsel

The regional communities maintain structures for the guarantee of the rights of all and for the exercise of authority with appropriate accountability between leaders and members (Constitutions § 77)

Rooted in God we are drawn into deeper bonds of friendship and reconciliation and are empowered for mission (Constitutions § 18)

19. The Church teaches that all the baptized, including those in consecrated life, have a right to due process, to appeal a decision that aggrieves them, to seek redress for wrongs, to defend themselves against accusations, and to have representation by

an advocate. To insure each Sister's right of representation, an annual budget of $100,000 shall be designated for use by members. Administered by the Reconciliation Board, this fund shall be made available when members wish to seek canonical counsel and pay a customary stipend to a lay or clerical advocate. Access to the fund shall be made by petition of an individual Sister to a member of the Reconciliation Board. A member's right to confidentiality in seeking canonical advice shall be rigorously respected. The Reconciliation Board shall maintain a list of qualified canonists.

Occasion for Seeking Canonical Counsel

Just as with a spiritual director or counselor, any Sister can seek canonical assistance. Occasions for seeking a clerical, religious, or lay canonist can include personal education or consultation, assistance with the Reconciliation Process, advocacy in ministry, or representation before regional or Institute leadership.

Elected and Appointed Officers

Each regional community through its chapter delineates the following in its regional directory . . . terms, roles, requirements and eligibility for office . . . " (Constitutions § 71)

The regional community chapter has policy-making authority subject to the Institute Constitutions, the acts of the Institute chapter and the policies of the Institute (Constitutions § 72)

Appointment to Incorporation Ministry

20. When a Mercy of the Burlingame Regional Community is appointed to Institute Incorporation Ministry, or her term comes up for renewal, a two-thirds vote of the Burlingame membership is required to approve/confirm the appointment or re-appointment. The vote is solicited by the RLT, and the result reported both to Burlingame members and the Institute.

Liaisons

21. Each regional community through its chapter delineates the following in its regional directory . . . the regional community governance structure and ways of amending it . . . terms, roles, requirements and eligibility for office." (Constitutions § 71)

- Liaisons are elected for a three-year term to coincide with the beginning and middle of a six-year term of office for the RLT. If the RLT is elected for a four-year term, the liaison will be elected for a coinciding four-year term. Liaisons are not reappointed by the RLT, but must be reelected by members by majority vote.

- A liaison's term of office expires with that of the RLT.

- Nominations and elections for new liaisons occur within the same Chapter as elections for the RLT.

- Liaisons receive their authority from the vote of the members, as Congresspersons receive their authority from the citizenry. The liaison represents a member's interests and concerns to leadership, serves as a mediator, and is the spokesperson, advocate, and ally of the member.

- As alternative to the liaison structure, or in addition, each Sister, from novice to first professed, from finally professed to semiretired, to retired, shall have the right to freely choose any finally professed Sister to act as her personal representative or agent for any specific purpose. The representative will act as the member's advocate in community relations, to see that her wishes are effectively communicated, her individual interests are preserved and her personal rights are diligently respected.

Term of Office of RLT

Each regional community through its chapter delineates the following in its regional directory . . . the regional community governance structure and ways of amending it . . . terms, roles, requirements and eligibility for office." (Constitutions § 71)

22. Term of office for elected leadership shall be restored to a four (4) year term.

Elections

23. The nomination and elections for offices of president and leadership team, liaisons, and Reconciliation Board members shall occur within the same Chapter session to preserve the right of members to discuss choices with each other face to face.

Medical Records of Sisters and Decisions about Medical Care

No one is permitted to damage unlawfully the good reputation that another person enjoys or to violate the right of another person to protect his or her own privacy. (Code of Canon Law §220)

Superiors are forbidden to induce their subjects in any way whatever to make a manifestation of conscience to them. (Code of Canon Law § 630.5)

Chapters and Sisters in positions of governance exercise authority in the Institute according to the universal law of the Church . . . (Constitutions § 51)

24. Ecclesial protections for members' privacy and California civil law regarding privacy of medical records shall be observed in relation to Sisters' employment and medical history. Provisions of civil law in relation to medications, treatment records, and physician-patient relations shall apply to the care of all community members, whether retired or not.

The Regional Leadership Team or their delegates shall not disclose or make use of any Sister's medical records without that Sister's personal authorization. No consultation with a Sister's physicians shall be made without the authorization of the Sister or her personal representative. Decisions about a Sister's medical care shall be made with her, not about her, and in consultation first with her and her personal representative.

No determination of a Sister's competency shall be made by leadership that is independent of a certification by her own, freely chosen physician.

Choice of Facility in Which to Retire

25. Sisters shall be provided a choice of retirement facility in addition to Marian Convent. The RLT shall conduct an anonymous survey of members about their preferences and reasons. Financial planning shall be adjusted accordingly.

Marian Care Center Administration

26. The daily operations, hiring of personnel and policies related to medical care of Sisters at Marian Care Center in Burlingame shall be reviewed and approved by a Board of Directors composed of medically qualified Sisters of Mercy.

Mercy Day

27. Celebration of September 24 at the Motherhouse shall be revised so its character as the patronal feast of the Sisters of Mercy will be evident to the vowed members. Currently, the day has come to be characterized as an Associates' commitment and renewal celebration.

Hospitality Subsidy for Vowed
Members at Mercy Center

We strive to witness to mercy when we reverence the dignity of each person, create a spirit of hospitality ... (Constitutions §8)

The administration of these temporal goods and the distribution of surplus funds are determined within the regional community and specified in directories or handbooks as appropriate. (Constitutions § 81)

28. Grateful to its members, the community encourages Sisters to enjoy each other's company at the Motherhouse and to find peace and rest there at any time. The Motherhouse, and within it Mercy Center, extends a spirit of welcome to all vowed members. To guarantee this hospitality, a subsidy of $50,000 (fifty thousand dollars) from Mercy Burlingame's general operating expenses shall be assigned annually to

Mercy Center's budget. This fund will pay for vowed members who visit the Motherhouse and wish to stay in rooms at Mercy Center. This hospitality subsidy covers Sisters who participate in Mercy Center programs, as well as Sisters who seek hospitality without program registration.

Procedure: A Sister secures a reservation from Mercy Center to assure availability of a room. On departure, she signs a form that lists the nights she stayed and meals she took on Mercy Center side. Mercy Center staff tallies these forms each quarter, and submits them to the Treasurer's Office for reimbursement from the Vowed Members Hospitality Subsidy Fund.

Ministry Advocate

As Sisters of Mercy we sponsor institutions . . . Within these institutions we . . . endeavor to model mercy and justice and to promote systemic change . . . (Constitutions §5)

We strive to witness to mercy when we reverence the dignity of each person (Constitutions § 8)

We do not, as members of a Religious Community, surrender our Christian responsibility to form our own conscience, to make moral judgments, or to act for the promotion of a just society. (Acts of Conscience Contrary to Civil Law, Policy Handbook III. E. 1)

29. The regional community shall designate a member of the RLT, a ministry coordinator or some other person to serve as community advocate for any Sister who asks for assistance with ministry- related contracts, supervisor-employee relations, evaluations, promotions, transfers, terminations or the like, especially in Mercy-sponsored institutions and Church-related settings. The advocate shall see that the Sister has access to professional resources to assist her negotiations, and to social support. By virtue of her being a vowed member, a Sister is entitled to the equivalent of "union representation" in the workplace.

Policies on Retirement and Residence
at Marian Care Center

Reverence for the unique gift of each member—the young and the old, the well and the infirm—helps us to live together in affection and mutual respect. (Constitutions §18)

Each regional and local community provides participative structures to afford its members the opportunity to influence the direction of their community and to shape its policies . . . (Constitutions 76)

In virtue of membership each Sister assumes the responsibility to participate in the decision making processes of the Institute, regional and local communities. (Constitutions § 78)

30. All relations of leadership with Sisters in retirement or in residence at Marian Care Center shall be characterized by a spirit of tenderness, affection, deference, and protectiveness, in respect and gratitude for our Sisters' long years of self-sacrifice and service. Thus, the RLT shall insure that

    ➤ The policy Retirement of Sisters (Handbook III. C. 1) is carefully observed

    ➤ That each Sister who wishes chooses her own liaison

    ➤ That each Sister who wishes appoints a personal representative

    ➤ That Sisters in residence be empowered to shape the policies at Marian

    ➤ That closed-circuit TV provide access to chapter and assembly meetings

    ➤ That a Bill of Patients' Rights be formulated to insure a grievance procedure at Marian in accord with the Joint Commission on Accreditation of Healthcare Organizations; Title 22, California Code of Regulations; and Medicare Conditions of Participation.

    ➤ To insure that Sisters have confidence in an emotionally safe setting, free from verbal or physical abuse, coercion, retaliation, or fear of denial of care.

Healing Services

When breaches of charity occur, we encourage each other to speak the truth in love and to bring prayer and patience to the restoration of harmony. (Constitutions §18)

31. The RLT will initiate the planning of optional healing services
    - to provide opportunity for members to speak the truth in love within the context of community itself,
    - to create a climate for acknowledgment and forgiveness
    - to bind up and balm the wounds we have inflicted on each other,
    - taking responsibility for past breaches of loyalty and love,
    - in conversion from habits of silence and disengagement
    - seeking to reconcile relationships and heal memories
    - to recover as Sisters our energy, joy, and trust in each other.

Survey of Challenges in Orienting Mercy's Reconciliation Board

(Prepared for Women's Commission
Sub-Committee Planning Meeting, Chicago)

This is a tentative analysis of the challenges:

1. Systemic Change

The project of education needed to use the process involves three audiences: 1) the Reconciliation Board; 2) Leadership; 3) Members at large. This involves the transmission and learning of new information in all three sectors.

2. Outcomes

Mercy has a God-inspired tradition, a viable mission, and faithful, generous women. These strengths are compromised by an internal spiritual culture that is neither healthful for human growth, nor attractive to prospective members. This is the general state of religious life. Establishment of internal appellate processes is essential to the revitalization of religious life. Different kinds of personal qualities for leadership will be trusted when the governance structure depends less on having leaders with personal traits of decency and kindness than a structure that itself assures accountability of leaders to members for their decisions and decision-making processes. Peace within community life is promoted by a common definition of ecclesial rights, along with a public, objective set of norms for fairness, and clear due process procedures whose aim is to protect entitlements of members, so that internal congregational governance reflects "integrity of word and deed in our lives." (Const. §8)

3. Specifying the Rights of Members

The basic insight that needs to be communicated is this: The same principles of dignity and equality we advocate "out there" for the poor, for women, and for those suffering discrimination apply also "in here" to vowed women in the congregation. Charity, justice, and peace apply as principles to the internal governance of the Institute and to the claim of individual members on fundamental rights. Whether a directive or decision is made by elected or delegated bodies, members first have a right that the content comply with universal and particular law. (CCI 1983 §617)

They also are entitled to have procedures aimed at protecting their equality of rights without discrimination, their right of defense against accusations prior to judgment, their right to seek redress for wrongs, their right to live their vowed life in peace and right relations with their Sisters, their right to canonical counsel, to objective decision-making procedures, to preservation of their good reputation, and to privacy in matters of conscience.

Correspondence to some rights can be found in the gentle, relational, and poetic provisions of the Constitution, e.g. "When breaches of charity occur, we encourage each other to speak the truth in love and to bring prayer and patience to the restoration of harmony" (Const. §18). However, in typical cases of dispute or conflict, such provisions exist as ideals, but in acknowledgment of human nature, need to be translated into community structures that support the ideal.

4. Integration of Concept of Rights into Theology of Religious Life

We acknowledge the ignorance of religious women about their rights, ignorance of leaders, and lack of structures that name or protect those rights. Regretfully, canon lawyers, whose advice is relied on by leadership, have failed in recent years to advise superiors about the rights of members, despite the fact that "rights language" is taken for granted within the guild of the Canon Law Society of America. The information needed to reform the Reconciliation Process is not available through retrieval of notes from formation conferences, reflection on personal experience, prayer, spiritual reading, brain-storming, Vatican II documents, the writings of current theologians, or even from Church documents about religious life. As analogy: The program has simply not been entered onto the hard drive of the community's consciousness, nor does it exist in the system as a shared or retrievable file.

The concepts related to rights, which apply to all persons in the Church, can be found in such sections of the 1983 Code as §§ 38, 48–58, 128 (compliance of administrative acts with Church law); §§ 208–223 (rights of all the faithful); §§ 1732–1739 (appeal of administrative decrees); and Book VIII (trials, due process). Application of these principles to women in religious life needs to be spelled out, and a treatment of vowed life rethought. A new Vatican document on religious life is needed to highlight these rights as entitlements for vowed women, and translate these rights into the governance, spirituality, and community life of vowed women with emphasis on practical social structures that protect rights, and duties of superiors in light of these assurances.

5. Present Reconciliation Process is Not Viable

The present reconciliation process is unworkable principally for two reasons:

a) The first unworkable term: The provision that decisions related to "membership" are not matters for the board. This leads to abuses by leadership, which can characterize any dispute as a matter of membership, i.e., the issue on the table is dismissal of a finally professed member because of her disobedience to a directive of the regional superior.

As for Sisters in first profession, this provision in the original Reconciliation Process violates a vowed member's rights under canon law to seek review of any decision that has aggrieved her and to exercise her right of defense. The provision was made for political reasons, to preserve the privilege of regional presidents having the sole and last word on not admitting a Sister in first vows to final profession, without a structure of accountability to anyone for her decision.

Such a practice is presently out of step with the Institute practice that many Sisters collaborate in the incorporation process, have journeyed with her through first vows and renewal. A structure already exists that protects the rights of a professed Sister seeking final vows, and provides a forum for the regional superior. This is the review process implied in Const. §67: "For the Institute president and the council to act validly in the dismissal of a professed Sister a collegial vote is necessary. The norms of the universal law are observed."

b) The second unworkable term: If one party refuses to participate, the process of conciliation or mediation stops. There is no recourse for a petitioner if the other party declines to participate; i.e., the process has no teeth because the opposite party (generally leadership) can opt out.

6. Fixing a Non-Viable Process

The present process can be modified by two important changes:
- a) All decisions affecting individuals, including "membership" are appropriate matter for the board.
- b) In cases where one party declines participation, the board continues the process on behalf of the petitioner first by investigation, then by composing a report that narrates the facts. This report is given to the petitioner so she can proceed to other levels or kinds of resolution, whether through the Institute, or through a diocesan tribunal.
- c) However, these changes are not sufficient to reform the process as part of Mercy's governance structure.
- d) The two modifications can be effected immediately to the Reconciliation Process by the ILT because it is canonically responsible to see that review processes are viable, no matter what form they take.

7. Acknowledging the Need for Change

The present reconciliation process is unworkable, both as a governance structure and as a viable appellate process and must be rethought from a systemic perspective.

The name "reconciliation" distracts from the fact that it should serve 1) as a formal appellate process for members to defend themselves when allegations are made about their conduct or character; 2) as a grievance procedure for members to deal with "perceived injustice" when they are given a directive ; 3) as true "reconciliation," which can be defined as the work of healing, peace making and restorative justice in

a) fostering charity in the community and right relations of members
b) taking means to fulfill the standard of Catherine McAuley: "the sun never went down on their anger," by offering processes to deal with grudges and shunning
c) seeking healing of mind, memory, and emotions for hurts to the community
d) providing a structure to memorialize and acknowledge historical truths even when the past can't be changed
e) providing alternatives to confrontational, adversarial communication
f) acknowledging that other parties other than disputants are affected by instances of "perceived injustice" and breakdown of communication
e) use of alternative dispute resolution through conciliation, mediation and arbitration of disputes
f) use of outside experts to assist these efforts when petitioner requests.

8. Balance of Powers as Principle of Democratic, Participative Governance

The Reconciliation Board is part of an appellate structure in an overall governance scheme that divides power, however unevenly, among executive, legislative and judicial. The "balance of powers" exists in the U.S. Constitutions, functions in the Church to protect the rights of individuals through diocesan tribunals, Rota, and Signatura. It exists *in potentia* in the governance structure of religious life. The mandate for the "balance of powers" comes from principles of international human rights, laws of democratic nations, and canon law as it applies to vowed members of religious communities. The origin of "balance of powers" is not internal to Mercy Constitutions, although its principles are illustrated there.

9. An Appellate Process is Not Left to Free Choice or Discernment

Vowed members enjoy two sets of ecclesial rights: those of the baptized and those specific to religious life. Establishing a workable grievance procedure and appellate process is not a matter left to the choice of a Mercy region, or to any religious congregation. As a pontifical congregation, the Institute must provide an appellate review process for leaders' decisions and directions. The review process is measured by its recognition of the dignity of each person, and a recognition of personal rights and due process as those are protected in the universal law of the Code of Canon Law. An internal review process must be provided by Mercy leadership to serve as an alternative to a diocesan tribunal because Mercy enjoys the privilege of self-governance as a pontifical congregation.

At the same time, Mercy members have a right as baptized and as laity to seek recourse through a diocesan tribunal. Vowed members can petition the Congregation for Religious to have a diocesan tribunal provide first instance review of decisions, redress for grievances, or restoration of right relations if neither the regional community nor the Institute provide adequate counsel, viable appellate structures, fair due process procedures, or prompt review.

10. Mercy's Constitutions Includes Provisions of Canon Law

One of the privileges of a pontifical congregation is that its internal governance processes are not subject to the authority of the local bishop. However, "authority to organize and govern ourselves" (Const. §52) does not mean independence from provisions of Canon Law, establish the Institute as an autonomous "church within a church," or make the personal directives of a regional superior equivalent to a papal directive. There are nearly twenty direct references to Church law in Mercy Constitutions, underlining the fact that this larger frame is the reference for members' rights and appellate procedures, even if all these provisions are not replicated in Mercy's Constitution.

11. Interference from the Culture of Blind Obedience: Compliance and Fear

The principal cultural conflict in making the reconciliation process truly functional is the culture and tradition of blind obedience, which underlies a leader's assumptions about the scope of her personal authority, a member's assumption about what the vow of obedience fundamentally requires, and community members' assumption about the power of its group decision (majority rule) over the lives of individual members.

A spiritual tradition of blind obedience is bedrock to religious life. Fear of "what will happen" if a member disobeys acts as a control over members' questioning of decision making by leadership. Discussion of appellate and grievance processes—by which members seek review of decisions and redress for grievances—can likely threaten leaders' and members' sense of life and order.

What if the vow of obedience, as traditionally understood and lived, collapses? Won't that unravel religious life? A corrected theology needs to be communicated, and "appellate" and "grievance procedure" and "rights" integrated with the concept of "discernment." Discernment is not fake conversation, but a process that theoretically can include accountability, review, and reversal. Discernment can embrace a sequence of discussions and testings, by which a member comes either to accept a decision made about her by a superior because it is affirmed, or to have it reversed after review at the appellate level.

12. The Alien Quality of "Rights" Language for Religious Women

"Rights" language is strongly resisted by some religious women as "secular," "legal," and "pre-Vatican." So is "canon law." Both are stereotyped as "patriarchal," "oppressively authoritarian," "alien to the spirit of community as family, " "male-made," or "not based in the gospel, the following of Jesus, or a female style of relating." This distaste needs to be acknowledged and an approach planned to deal with it.

13. The Discernment Mode, Administrative Norms, and Appellate Processes

For at least three decades, "discernment," a term borrowed from the Spiritual Exercises of St. Ignatius, has been migrating from its original context, the making of a personal vocational choice and decision about ministerial service, to a variety of other contexts. These include the congregation's election of community leaders and the facilitation of formal assembly processes. "Discernment mode" in congregational assemblies is associated with a prayerful context, calm reflection, a reading of the mood and emotions of the group, response of the process to opinions and straw votes by the group, and constant adjustment of the process to change in the flow of direction manifest by the participants.

In other words, the discernment mode is subjective, unpredictable, and subject to constant change as retuning is made by the facilitator. The discernment mode rests on the assumption that external rigid rules do not govern the delicacy of how the Holy Spirit may inspire the group. Thus "the rules" will be made as the processing proceeds, and by group consensus in agreeing to changes.

In orienting leadership to the function of a Reconciliation Board, the culture of the discernment mode needs to be distinguished from a "due process" model. Discernment mode suggests to elected leaders that one of their roles as a leader-facilitator is to formulate new rules, adjust procedures and change congregational policies in response to an ever changing communal subjectivity. By contrast, "due process" might seem an alien concept, since it describes the accountability of leadership to a framework of existing, objective norms which are not subject to the discernment mode: canon law, civil law, Mercy Constitutions, Directory, and published congregational policies and procedures. There is a collision between "discernment mode" culture and accountability to standard administrative and management practices. Discernment mode is not the equivalent of an identifiable and predictable governance structure.

The reconciliation process serves an appellate function within a governance structure. It measures directives and decisions of leadership against objective content of existing laws. It tests the matter of a grievance for a leader's or delegated body's compliance with common, generally applicable procedures and principles of due process.

The subjectivity of a discernment mode process puts at risk the guarantee that all members will be treated equally. The Reconciliation Board exists as check and balance—that decision-making processes affecting individual members will follow criteria for fairness that can be measured against publicly stated procedures, and will have a content that can be tested for resonance with universal and particular law. Expecting fair procedures for decision making, which apply to all persons at all times, is not "legalistic" but standard management practice for leaders of companies and organizations.

This clarification is made more necessary by the fact that many Sisters in the leadership pool have had no academic training in organizational management or human services and no experience in acting as a CEO in a non-Mercy institution. Their leadership experience has been limited to roles within the Institute where they are accountable only to other Mercies. A process for effective facilitation of meetings in the discernment mode does not insure fair practices by executives in all other areas of management.

14. Conceptual Gaps to Fill and Make the Reconciliation Process More Coherent

There are several conceptual gaps among women religious—lack of information and knowledge—regarding major developments that have impacted the status and named the rights of women over the last fifty years:

a) The effect of WW II on subsequent legislation of international law defining human rights and women's rights beyond the provisions for rules of war under Geneva Conventions.

b) The Civil Rights movement in the U.S. of the 1960s, which resulted in federal antidiscrimination legislation for women and minorities. Subsequent state and federal law has rewritten the status of women in the U.S. During the 1960's, attention of religious women was focused on liturgical reform and updating of lifestyle for religious as part of Vatican II's *aggiornamento*. Religious women do not have an intellectual frame that identifies them with all women whose status has changed in society.

c) In 1983, the revised Code of Canon Law was promulgated. However, Mercy membership was never oriented to its liberating provisions. Instead, membership retains general distaste for canon law based on associations with the 1917 Code, in effect for 90 percent of the Congregation when they went through formation.

d) The secular feminist movements of the 1920s in Europe and the 1970s in the U.S. had some effect on women's religious life, but also created alienation between laywomen and vowed women. Part of this alienation was the result of secular feminists' endorsement of contraception and abortion, contrary to the Roman Catholic moral teaching. Vowed women have not thought through the competing loyalties: expressing solidarity with all women, yet expressing compliance with the Church's official doctrine.

15. Anthropology of the Vowed Woman: Believer, Vowed, Citizen

One myth that underlies vowed women's sense of disempowerment is the supposed division between baptism as a believer and secular identity as a citizen. If a vowed woman belongs to God, she doesn't belong to Caesar. Part of vowed women's resistance to the concept of having "rights" is related to an assumption that vows abrogate civil rights, or that by making vows, a woman gives up most of her rights as a citizen as part of her sacrifice of self. The concept of her rights in the Church has not been integrated into an understanding of religious life and vows.

The concept of the "citizen-believer" needs to be incorporated into the concept of what it means to be a woman with vows in the Church. She is simultaneously a believer and a citizen, as well as a vowed woman. She has a triple identity. Myths about the "separation of Church and state" also need to be challenged—an assumption that if a religious belongs to the Church, she has "left the world," and separated herself from the state. She may assume that state law doesn't apply to her, only Church law. The implication of a theology of rights on the living of vows is a needed development in the spirituality of religious life.

16. Culture and Virtue of Silence

We have inherited a spiritual culture of virtue that women suffer and mourn in silence and gain merit by doing so; we have inherited a social culture as women not to be angry, but rather to accept suffering. Irish Catholic social values, Mercy's human and cultural heritage, have also legitimated "not talking about it" if: a) topics are likely to result in a dispute; or b) are "not things we discuss in public." The reconciliation process as an appellate structure challenges the culture of silence. There is a structure for making a petition so that a matter that has been hurtful or unjust will be talked about and reviewed, not kept secret or suppressed. There is a structure to lessen hurt, reduce anger, and restore peace.

17. Reconciliation Process as Imposition of the Institute on Regions

Some confusion exists about the reconciliation process as an Institute process imposed on the regions, and one that involves loss of autonomy of regions over their own self-governance. The history of the reconciliation process needs to be reviewed, along with distinguishing which regions/provinces had formal grievance or reconciliation processes in place, and which ones did not.

18. Primarily Ecclesial Role of Reconciliation Board

The board's responsibilities are first ecclesial, second, congregational. This orientation is needed to empower boards with a correct sense of their place and authority in the Church and in the Institute governance structure. Board members are not appointed, but elected because they belong to the official governance structure democratically chosen by community members.

Because of a lack of orientation to their place and role, some members of the board may feel that their community relations will be compromised because they might "go against" a Sister in elected office and be retaliated against later. Sisters who cannot act autonomously as members of a review board should not stand for service. A Sister petitioner who fears her regional Reconciliation Board is not competent enough, or not autonomous enough, can present her petition to another region's board, or can petition at the Institute level.

19. Congregational Moment.

The Institute is in a reorganization process, and one outcome will probably involve a loss of intimacy and familiarity between leaders and members in some mergings. When leaders have no personal history with members, an appellate process is a protection, both for leaders and members, so that decision making can be reviewed to insure they are based on accurate and complete information, that both sides have been heard, and fair procedures have been followed.

20. Citing Authoritative Sources for a Reconciliation and Grievance Process

While the process is mentioned in regional directories, no clear reference to a grievance or appellate processes exists in the Constitution except in Const. §65 where the President will "serve as an instance of appeal." This is canonical shorthand, and its implications need to be spelled out more fully by canonists who can explain "instance" as an official level of ecclesial review.

Scripturally, the process is grounded in the role of the Holy Spirit, the example of Jesus, themes of forgiveness, justice, peace, correction of faults, defense of the accused, healing, pastoral tenderness of leaders, love of friends for each other, preference for means other than civil litigation to resolve disputes, and restoration of right relations, both in the Hebrew and Christian texts.

Sacramentally, the opening rite of the Eucharist provides an occasion to acknowledge wrongdoing that injures others. The revised Rite of Reconciliation is a model, where confession is made and absolution is received both individually and generally. Less attractively because of its trivialization, the former practice of Chapter of Faults had as its original purpose to keep the peace among persons living at close quarters, allowing ritual clearing of the air for conduct that was not sinful, but socially hurtful or offensive.

There is decline in regularity of the Eucharist and Sacrament of Reconciliation because of the priest shortage, along with absence of paraliturgical rituals for acknowledgment of faults and extending of forgiveness within community. Sadly, a "grand silence" in which disagreeing Sisters cease to speak to each other, has become more normative than active practices for promoting reconciliation and restoration of peace among members. The liturgical vacuum increases the urgency for the Institute to provide supportive structures for maintaining Mercy's spiritual life and tradition of trustful, affectionate relations among Sisters. The need to heal old wounds, both individual and corporate, will impede any effective re-imagining or reorganization of the Institute. The effective functioning of a Reconciliation Board can decrease the likelihood of perpetuating the pain members bear.

21. ILT Responsibility to Maintain and Supervise Appellate Structures

Under Const. §65, where the president will "serve as an instance of appeal," the president and ILT are responsible to see that viable and operational first instance appellate structures exist at the regional level. They have the responsibility to see that a board is called at the Institute level, to serve either as a first or second instance of appeal for members. The president, in the present scheme of the reconciliation process, can act personally or with the council as a first instance of appeal for a member who asks for review of a regional superior's directive. Additionally, acting personally or with the council, the Institute president can serve as a second instance of appeal from either a regional board, or the Institute board.

The main purpose of the structure is to protect the rights of members who do not have personal power or authority equal to a superior in elected office. A vowed member's right of appeal is compromised if the Institute president permits elected regional leaders to make accusations about a Sister or engage in one-sided consultations with her about lower level decisions or directives affecting individual Sisters. If the Sister affected is left out of the consultation, her right of defense and right of appeal to the president are effectively nullified.

Such practices rob members of their rights, and reinforce the culture of blind obedience in which a member submits without protest to whatever the superior directs, no matter whether its content is based on legitimate grounds or personal preference.

22. Maintaining Separate Slates of Consultants for Region and Institute

In order to preserve her personal responsibility to serve as an instance of appeal, the Institute president must have structures and consultants in place who keep her free from entanglement in lower-level decision-making processes. Inconsistent with her constitutional responsibility is allowing regional superiors to "consult her" prior to their giving directives to members, on the model of a high school teacher consulting with the principal before the teacher takes disciplinary action against the students.

To avoid conflicts of interest, care must be taken that consultants to the Institute president are not also advising regional superiors in a matter that is likely to be the subject of a grievance or a review process. It would be more protective of members' rights to have canonical advocates, for example, assigned to advise board members at the regional level. These should be distinguished from advocates whose service will be exclusive to Institute board.

23. Regional Superiors and Institute President

In Const. §77, "The regional communities maintain structures for the guarantee of the rights of all."

It is the responsibility of the Institute president to keep in place structures that hold regional superiors accountable to Church law, due process, and objective procedures. The right of members to seek the Institute president as an instance of review is compromised if the president becomes party to directives given by a regional superior to a member of her region.

The right to appeal to the Institute president belongs to the member, not to a regional superior wishing to secure her authority to act against a member, as in a military model. The distinction between executive and juridical functions of the Institute president's office need to be kept clear, as acknowledgment and protection of a member's rights.

24. Subsidiarity and Hierarchy

The administrative principle of "subsidiarity" refers to a "higher up" manager letting lower-level decisions be made by administrators at that level, as a more efficient and fair practice. This is opposed to the undesirable dynamic of "centrism" in which the highest authority seeks to centralize power and resolve lower-level matters "from the top." By contrast, in a balance-of-powers model, a juridical or semi-juridical process is hierarchical, and works in just the opposite fashion, from lower to higher.

"Subsidiarity" is a separate concept, belonging to administrative and executive practice. A reverse-hierarchical process of grievance or review goes from lower to higher level. Structures for the higher level of Institute review structures must be in place and function in a "clean" way, uncompromised or tainted by prior consultation with regional superiors. The interplay of subsidiarity and hierarchy needs to be developed as orientation for leadership.

25. Two-Day Format for Meeting: Educational Content and Process Training

Day One: Content and Education

The presentation of the information can involve lectures, charts, slides, role-plays and can involve both seriousness and humor. However, the genre is not a retreat, but a continuing education, content-oriented workshop. I propose two days. First is to do the historical, scriptural, ecclesial, psychological, and canonical education and integrate a concept of rights into the understanding of who is the person of the woman who makes vows, and where are the sources of her multi-faceted identity and her rights (baptism, vows, citizenship).

Pedagogical Topics for Orientation

The information can be organized pedagogically as grounded in :

1) concept of human dignity and human rights as applied to vowed women
2) principles of charity, peace, and justice as applied to vowed women
3) the scriptures, both OT and NT on justice, forgiveness, restitution, conflict resolution, various leadership styles for promoting these
4) the juridical tradition of individual rights in Roman law to which the Church fell heir
5) provisions of the 1983 Code of Canon Law and Church law applied to Mercy leaders and members
6) Mercy's Constitution and direction statements on justice-peace-rights themes
7) Citizenship in a democratic state, U.S. Constitution and civil rights harmonious with vows
8) Feminist theology and secular feminist reform movements; women's rights.

Day Two: Processes for Petitions Received by Reconciliation Board

A training, given through case studies, role-playing, sample texts, will be designed to treat practicalities of the process—the nuts and bolts.

Board members will learn approaches for each of the three "occasions":

1) Juridical: exercising the right of defense when a member has been directly or indirectly accused of an act of wrong- doing, or failing "to be a good nun";

2) Grievance: asking for a review of a directive or decision by leadership (elected or delegated), affecting her personally; this includes the right to due process, petitioning for a review of the procedure that was followed in giving the directive;

3) Reconciliation: seeking redress for wrongs, restoration of right relations when there are breaches of charity between members.

Theories of Justice as the Basis for the Reconciliation Process

In devising processes for each function of a Reconciliation Board, a foundation should be laid by outlining various theories of justice so that board members have a common understanding of where their strategies for peace making might be grounded. These include the interplay of: 1) just practices grounded in conformity with positive law; 2) justice measured by its utility for the good of society or order for the greater number of people; 3) justice as the realization of individual rights within a scheme of mutuality of rights, based on "natural law" written in the heart of each person by the Creator.

If there is "no peace without justice," the theoretical orientation includes a treatment of justice as an outcome for all parties in which there is a balancing among: 1) a subjective perception or "feel" of fairness; 2) a distribution of resources or outcomes in which each party gets a share; 3) a procedure and process that has been fair.

Further, the work of the Reconciliation Board is distinguished from the adversarial culture of civil (or ecclesial) litigation. The board can function in a quasi-juridical role in dealing with some petitions, such as one member's accusation against a Sister of noncriminal conduct which is nonconformity with the norms of being a "good religious." However, its role is not to conduct a trial, but protect the member's rights by testing the content of the accusation for validity against canon law, Constitutions, Directory, and congregational policies.

The board provides a structure in which the accused can memorialize her defense. It examines the kind of evidence, conduct, and procedure of the Sister who brought the accusation. Thus, the board in its quasi-juridical role preserves the right of a member to due process. Its role is to provide a forum for discourse and resolution, and the restoration of right relations.

In matters of reviewing decisions and in working to restore right relations, the exercise of prudential judgment in testing directives against universal and particular law is distinguished from a trial process. A review of a regional superior's directive to a member undergoes an appellate process. This means that a member has exercised her right to appeal a decision that has aggrieved her to the board. As an appellate body, the board receives a member's request to reexamine a decision that she feels harms her, is unjust or illegitimate in its content, or one that did not issue from a fair, objective process.

Consultants and Ongoing Education of Board Members

1. Board members may recognize that they lack competence in a particular area, e.g., reviewing a leader's directive or decision for its compliance with Canon Law. Policies for use of consultants, theologians, canon lawyers, civil lawyers, both within Mercy and outside the Institute, need to be developed.

- Board members are expected to engage in continuing education, develop peace-making skills, and enlarge a repertoire of alternative dispute resolution procedures.
- Models of grievance procedures exist in our sponsored health care institutions and can be adapted for use by boards.
- Other congregations have developed grievance procedures and a pool of them can be created through Leadership Council for Women Religious.
- A broad slate of canon lawyers, religious, lay, female, and male should be developed to assist regions, both members and leaders. The canon lawyers should be vetted by an Institute review board for their understanding of religious life, their advocacy of women's equality in Church and society, their commitment to the rights of members, their

educational background and areas of ministerial expertise, theological perspective, resonance with Mercy values and good standing in the Church.

An ad hoc committee should interview canonists—diocesan-based, academically-based, or independent—and draw up a biographical paragraph to individualize them as advocates, provide resources for each region of the country, and circulate this list to all members of the Institute.

Communication to Members

Text revisions of the reconciliation process will be communicated to each member of the Institute, both leaders and members, possibly as a booklet.

Ongoing education of Sisters in leadership can be incorporated into Institute Leadership Council meetings.

Comments on "With a Passion for Christ and Passion for Humanity"

(Working Paper for the Congress on Religious Life,
Sponsored by the International Union of Superiors
General [UISG], Rome, Italy)

Introduction: Underlying Tensions about Church and Culture

The working paper for the Congress on Religious Life of 2004 reflects a tension between two views of the Church and culture embedded in the documents of Vatican II: that of *Lumen Gentium* (LG, 1964) and *Gaudium et Spes* (GS, 1965). It would be fruitful to review not only the tone of the synod's *Vita Consecrata*, (VC) but also the themes of GS or *Church in the Modern World* to identify some fundamental lines of debate represented in "Passion for Christ and Passion for Humanity." (PCPH)

Thematic History

In LG, the Church is a tradition founded on the life of Jesus Christ in the New Testament, an orderly, hierarchical institutional structure that is witness to the world and stands as a light to the present culture, as a unique entity, with its own reality and integrity. This is the context for religious life, identified as a particular following of Jesus in the gospel, to carry out the mission of Christ in the world. Mary represents the culmination of what the Church means.

In GS, the orientation is slightly different. There is no particular treatment of priesthood and religious life. The people of God are the Church, and Church is identified with the hopes and sufferings of humanity. The Church exists on earth, within human culture. The dignity of the person, equality, moral conscience, human responsibility for the earth and for society, the problem of atheism, and what the Church receives from society are themes.

In VC, the first two drafts met with resistance from religious women because the message and tone seemed dictatorial. Endorsement of unity around fundamental spiritual values seemed an effort to roll back reforms of the period of Vatican II, and to revive a pre-Vatican spirit of intellectual submission to Church teaching and ministerial direction.

The final and revised version of VC was a transformed message, perhaps the fruit of a new committee. Nevertheless, the document recorded unresolved tensions among the writers in at least two different theologies of the vows. The final issue of VC was a tonal break with the drafts. It was a comparatively sunny, optimistic document, expressing gratitude for the diversity of charisms in religious life, confidence that religious would carry out their mission of evangelization within culture, while both affirming and encouraging the many ways religious could be "experts in communion" with cultures and other religious traditions.

The debate in PCPH reflects these multiple views of Church and the consequent tension around whether the present sociopolitical culture is good or bad, friend or foe of religious life. A question for discussion might be posed: Which reflection on the Church and which context for religious life unleashes the most energy at the present time?

The answer is a pragmatic matter, not whether one version of the Church is true and the other false. The evangelists Luke and John each found it necessary to retell and rewrite the story of Jesus of Nazareth for their own communities of faith, each in different locations with different social, political challenges. John's gospel "politics" reinforces the idea that the community of faith remains loyal to its personal dialogue with Jesus, and exists in a world that is hostile to the Word, rejects the Truth and resists the Spirit. Luke-Acts takes a different view of earthly culture, more accommodating and engaged, portraying Jesus urged on by the Spirit, with his disciples in Acts taking the message "to the ends of the earth."

These gospels exist simultaneously as testaments of faith, even though they are very different from each other. Pluralism in the views of Jesus, as separate and unique records, is the truth of the New Testament, not a reductionism and synthesis of all gospels into one story. The existence of the four gospels expresses in its own way the truth that: "The tendency toward a single way of thinking and the leveling of everything causes great tension and distress." (PCPH, V).

Voices in the Working Paper

I hear several distinct voices in this document:

1) The optimistic, affirming voice of religious life, like that of VC, looking at the future optimistically, calling on attendees to hear and promote newness, trusting that bringing women and men together is a new and prophetic moment. This voice encourages dialogue and communion with Scripture, culture, other congregations, and between men and women, confident that new ideas will be heard, and creating a tone of welcome for that diversity. It encourages proposals that will help "restructure, innovate and rethink our concrete actions." It speaks of the Church as a "sacrament of humanization." It takes pride in using the instruments of modern communication—Web site, e-mail—to open involvement and promote exchange worldwide on the topic of religious life.

2) The voice, like that of LG, that says the problems in religious life call for a renewal of personal spirituality, purifying of vision, and a struggle with a culture whose values are alien to the Church's mission. This is a more judgmental voice, saying we must maintain the mission of the Church and think about the world, but reject its secularism and neoliberalism.

3) The voice that says that religious life will be renewed if members engage the world, take risks, overcome fear, go out from institutions and serve the poor, oppressed, and marginalized more energetically (GS). This voice, however, has a note of "try harder" and ignores what has already been done as "not yet enough." It deflects a sense of accomplishment or reliance of religious on their institutional apostolates. It blames religious for being too conformist culturally, ministerially focused too narrowly, and politically conservative.

4) The voice of realism, which is ready to acknowledge obstacles and distinct problems that cause religious life not to prosper in the Church: cultural dominance of men over women, the sexual abuse scandals, affective immaturity of members, aging of mem-

bers, intolerance of diversity within religious life, a closed ecclesi-astical system, authority's suppression of prophetic efforts by those in consecrated life, that this is not the best hour of religious life, that there are abuses of power in religious life, that members have failed to offer friendship and support to each other in light of the new anthropology, and a need for other forms of government and organization (PCPH, 38–40).

5) The politically correct voice, which minimizes problems and imposes "Vaticanese" discretion on the document in the form of gen-eralities like "certain circumstances" and "some places." It restrains the naming of problems directly, and censors themes such as the chal-lenges to religious life in an age of terrorism, intolerance of the Arab world toward the west, postcolonial hostilities, the changed role of women in the world, denial of their rights, physical and sexual vio-lence against women as a gender, and the form this takes in patriar-chal abuses of power and sexual exploitation of religious women by priests. This is the voice that ignores the agenda of the United Nations regarding women's rights and other projects representing the gospel mission of the Church, as though the Church is the only force capable of responding to the poor and oppressed.

Gender Roles and this Congress

One fundamental question is how much gender is controlling the content of PCPH. Is it recreating the paradigm that men in the Church speak authoritatively about concepts like postmodernity, politics, philosophy, theology, and doctrine while women just lis-ten? Would women, who outnumber male religious three to one, speak to each other in these voices and categories? Are women religious destined to speak primarily of their experience and per-sonal spiritual reflections?

Is this dialogue about religious life liberated from, or simply replicating the husband-wife roles of a 1950s marriage, in which assigned attitudes and expectations replicate unexamined social constructs governing the relations between men and women? How possible is true equality of discourse when the sacramental power to forgive sins, administer last rites, and preside at Eucharist is held, in our tradition, by religious men, making religious women spiritually dependent on them as an article of faith? Are the restrictions of the *burka* and the code of the Taliban outside or inside this Congress?

The Document's European Perspective: Is Rejection of Modern Culture Helpful?

The writers acknowledge it would be alien to the tradition of religious life to suppose that the congress could reduce all experience of religious life to one philosophical ideology, one cultural perspective, or one political agenda. A European academic perspective governs the section on "Challenges and Opportunities," especially the overview of globalization, unjust economic systems, postmodernism and secularist materialism (capitalism). These themes offer a certain political view, but this needs a critique from a non-European intellectual perspective.

For example, the "neoliberal" agenda of Europe, which promotes sober reexamination of previously established truths in light of WW II (post-modernism), less political power for the Church, divorce, reproductive rights, a secularized Constitution for the European Parliament, open immigration policies, global commerce—this is held suspect. At the same time, in Central and South America, a "neoliberal" agenda would mean a critique of the Church's complicity in maintaining the power of oppressive governments in El Salvador, Chile, Argentina; endorsement of liberation theology, advocating for the rights of women and indigenous people, and bringing former dictators to international tribunals for crimes.

These themes are also a casting of problems that men pose to women out of a male-dominated university academic perspective. What would African religious communities say? What of Asian religious who are minorities in nations without a Christian history? Are we all at war, worldwide, with every secular and political structure as it presently exists?

These sections reflect distrust of modernity, and suggest the triumphal outlook toward post-WW II culture of LG. To accept analyses of these sections in PCPH uncritically will reinforce an impulse that religious life must stand against the world, resist the platforms of capitalistic democratic governments, and carry out the mission of the Church as David against Goliath. The query, "Can any good come from Nazareth?" might be analogized here as the suspicion, Can any good come out of western democratic governments? Out of the United Nations?

Thus, the "Challenges and Opportunities" critique in PCWH (§ 17–44) needs an intellectual and philosophical review in light of the country where religious are serving. Are they citizens of the country where they mission? Or are they from the "outside?"

At present, PCPH seems to offer its own perspective as the equivalent of a new politicized spirituality for religious life. This perspective does not seem to take account of the different personal and spiritual realities represented by whether members are citizens, noncitizens, or regarded as colonialists in the countries where they minister; whether they are members of the ethnic and cultural majority or whether they are "foreigners" and minorities in the dominant culture. Is having secular identity as a citizen a constitutive, essential element of religious life, an accidental dimension, or an irrelevant one?

A spirituality of religious life, suitable for each setting, arises out of these varied cultural and political realities. This section of PCPH does not speak to the opportunities represented by enculturation or ecumenism, so perhaps the conversation at the congress will develop these themes.

The response of Marie Antoinette Saade, S.F.M. (Lebanon), all the more poignant because of its brevity, exemplifies, for example, a spirituality of survival in an ecclesially and politically compromised secular setting. The situation of religious women in Lebanon has been burdened by fourteen years of civil war, resentment by Arabs against French colonial history, competing interests of rival religious- political factions, Middle Eastern terrorist groups, effective military occupation by Syria, and divisions among Catholics themselves—Maronite, Roman Catholic, and Greek Orthodox. Saade herself does not speak of this real-life context, but acknowledges the "net of obstacles which never ends," and the "inextricable problems" whose hoped-for solutions may be as small as grains of sand, so small they don't attract attention.

She likely speaks for thousands of other religious women, including those at risk of violence and death at the hands of insurgents and militants. The danger in which they minister does not seem at the forefront of PCPH writers' consciousness.

Re-Reading the Samaritan Woman in John 4

A welcome invitation in PCWH is to explore "new and unthought . . . horizons" in reflecting on two icons, the story of the Samaritan woman (John 4:1–42) and the Good Samaritan (Luke 10:25–37).

Of all the respondents' papers posted at the Web site, the most eloquent rereading of the Samaritan woman dialogue is offered by Antonieta Potente, O.P. of Bolivia. ("Algunos apuntes alrededor del poso y por el camino"). Doing a mythical and symbolic reading, she finds a place for every detail in suggesting that this story describes both the world of religious life and of mission. For example, the midday heat connotes the weariness of our historical moment, our unfulfilled dreams, the time we feel sadness, and disillusion. The jug represents tradition—what it is like to be enculturated and conditioned as a woman, as an alien, as a Samaritan, as a Jew. The well of Jacob, Mount Gerazim, the road all have a place in the story of the woman and Jesus, in the story of religious life and of the mission.

However, an important insight is that the encounter of Jesus and the Samaritan is a story recovered, something itself alive, both within the person and in the mission. Life is revised by an encounter, and everything acquires significance because of a readiness for encounter. The nature of this encounter provides not only a perspective on life, but a way of encountering history, other individuals, and other peoples. The well is not only the location of tradition, or a place with cultic symbolism. Persons themselves are wells, places of profound revelation, guardians of secrets and living stories. Potente's reading is inclusive, trusting of culture in a pluralistic reality, and reflects the optimism of VC in proposing that religious become "experts in communion" with all aspects of that culture.

Here, it may also be well for me to note that PCPH §§ 61–64 relies on some traditional readings of the Samaritan woman that have become taken for granted as exegetical truth. Such presuppositions require revision in light of a feminist perspective as "new and unthought of horizons." This is because the demeaning way men think of the Samaritan woman suggests an attitude the institutional Church will bring to its discourse about women religious. The way the Samaritan woman is rendered in exegesis will be appropriated as part of religious women's own system of internal oppression.

Not a Sinner

First, there is no reason to suppose that the Samaritan woman in John 4 is a sinner, nor that Mary Magdalene in John 20 is either. The stock characterization of both women as having a "shady past" is that they are sexually weak, morally deviant prostitutes, reformed by their meeting with Jesus. Such an exegetical anthropology has been confirmed in decades of clerical preaching and male-dominated exegesis. However, the "shady past" exegesis demeans women, and confirms in the mind of believers, including women themselves, that their sexual nature is the source of sin, weakness, and shame and must be redeemed, and that passionate love for human beings cannot be trusted; only love for Jesus. There is no discussion of forgiveness in John 4, because the account is not about a woman's sinfulness, but her powerful witness.

Did Jesus choose women with shady pasts to rescue them? Is that the only reason they are credible? Is this gospel portrait the image of religious women that men in the Church cherish?

Meaning of Midday

Second, the reason the woman comes at midday to the draw water is not her wish to avoid the townsfolk out of shame. If she were so ashamed and marginalized, how is it that she has such immediate credibility with the townspeople right afterwards, when they come out of the city to him? (4:30). This "shame" exegesis ignores the symbolic function of time in John and the meaning of Jesus as revelation for every hour. Just as the teacher Nicodemus came to Jesus by night (3:1) and Jesus revealed himself despite the darkness using images of birth. Even so, in the full light of day Jesus also communicates who he is. The seven exchanges between Jesus and the woman allude to the Genesis creation of the world in seven days. Like the creation story in which God finds each day good, the Samaritan woman's conversation with Jesus should evoke a similar affirmation of gratitude and wonder as her story is elicited and her humanity affirmed by Jesus.

Such a reading avoids the prurient psychologizing of a woman supposedly "found out" by the prophet Jesus who proves he is divine by exposing her shameful failure in sustaining long-term commitments to men. Logically it makes no sense that the Samaritan woman reported that Jesus clairvoyantly exposed her secret sins and this made her feel such joy she went running to the public square to tell everyone. How did exposure of her secret sexual sins establish any credibility with townsfolk? Is there another more logical interpretation of, "Come, see a man who told me all that I ever did"?

What is it about these women's histories and personalities that make them ideal evangelists? The Samaritan woman, like Magdalene, is first a witness to a direct encounter with Jesus. What is utterly transformative for first-century hearers is that their society, like that of modern Afghanistan, assigned rights according to gender. Among the Taliban of the 1990s, women did not speak in public, were forbidden to be educated or to hold a job and had no authoritative voice to interpret the tradition. They were to cover their bodies from head to toe with a veil and conceal their personal identities.

Yet here in John's gospel, the Samaritan and Magdalene appear in public, prove themselves engagingly conversational and relational individuals. They turn out to be powerful teachers and credible messengers who evangelize others—men and women alike. Midday, in John 4, is the time when women come into their own, when they reveal themselves and throw off the oppression of the burka and the anonymity of the chador.

Like a rereading and corrected exegesis, religious life is in need of a rereading in light of a corrected anthropology about women's dignity and equality in the Church, in relation to clerics and laymen alike.

The Dialogue: Telling and Hearing, Asking and Answering

The most significant feature of John 4 is that it is the longest one-on-one dialogue in the New Testament. The dialogue with the

Samaritan woman displaces a more traditional theology and spirituality that attempt to locate religious women's reflection about their ecclesial identity on Mary the mother of Jesus. The Samaritan woman is the focus in John's gospel, not Mary of Nazareth. The governing questions, as analogy to reform of religious life, are: What quality of dialogue is it? What do the woman and Jesus talk about? What does a good relationship look like, if this dialogue is a model?

P. Gonzales Silva, C.M.F. ("Bases for Debate for the Congress") proposes that "Consecrated Life (CL) is in search of an encounter with Jesus . . . It presupposes an enlightened and compassionate encounter with the human, cultural, social and religious realities of the present age . . . being reborn into the socio-cultural and religious context of today."

The conventional interpretation of the Samaritan woman, governing §§61–62, is that she "bears in her heart a history of wounded relationships." A premise of her sexual adventures or victimhood as a pre-Hollywood star in "Pretty Woman," requires a somewhat magical transformation by story's end. From prostitute, she changes clothes and transforms herself into completely new person, disconnected from her malaise, emotional emptiness, and sexual misadventures of shameful loves. Her makeover complete, she rushes back to town, a morally converted and reformed missionary finally capable of evangelization.

What is an alternative, more coherent meaning of the woman's annunciation, "Come, see a man who told me all that I ever did" (4:29). I asked adult laywomen students what could account for a series of her attempted commitments. They suggested a different scenario: That one man might have been a wife beater or alcoholic, so she left; another might have been a soldier who went to war and never came home; a third might have become sick and died, leaving her a widow; a fourth, an adulterer, incapable of fidelity; a fifth might have discarded her, accusing her of barrenness if he was sterile and could not have children.

This alternative scenario, true to many women's collective experience, alters the exegetical caricature of her as a seductress and counters the moral assumption that all her life choices are a matter of will power. Such a misogynist anthropology needs to be replaced by educating men about women's social history and a psychology suited for 2004. Seminary education and religious formation should replace contempt by fostering empathy for each woman as a human person who has dignity, entitlement to make choices of her own, and the intelligence, courage and skill to carry out a destiny that is hers.

"Come See a Man Who Told Me Everything I Ever Did"

In an alternative reading of John 4, when Jesus says, "Go, call your husband, and come here" (4: 16), he indicates he does not intend to take sexual advantage of her, that he respects her integrity and commitments. When she says, "I have no husband," what subject does the dialogue turn to? The reflective reader empathizes with the Samaritan's life-long effort to establish lasting relationships. The reader imagines Jesus as a respectful counselor and friend. He opens his heart to her, welcomes her confidences with respect, and listens for a long time to the woman's disclosure of her story—the most personal aspects of her life. She feels like confiding to him the long story of her sadness and happiness, her efforts to love again and again, and all the good she has managed to accomplish in her life, despite the loneliness, obstacles, disappointments, and reversals. She shows who she is, the whole truth.

At the end, she admits she has given up on the formalities of marriage, but still believes mutuality and equality in love are possible. She has not given up on life, but is ready to risk and commit herself again, and will let go of the past with its disappointments. She tells Jesus what she thinks, what she believes, what she hopes for, what she loves, the meaning she finds in life, the good she still hopes to do.

As she has been telling Jesus her story, she feels joy and energy rise up in her, the hope of the life force itself, a flowing water from within her soul, of desire and willingness to love again, to extend herself to others. Jesus receives her confidences, reverences the disclosure, affirms her triumphs and personal strength, manifests his appreciation of her energy, admires her for what she has been through, and responds by sharing who he is.

Summing up everything she has told him as a worthy and admirable narrative, and confirming that he hears and believes her story, he says, "You have spoken rightly." In the Greek, this connotes admiration and approval of her accomplishment. Jesus communicates he has been listening to her and empathizes with her: "You have not had a man who was husband to you. You have indeed had five husbands and the one you now have is not your husband. You have spoken the truth to me."

Again, the Greek suggests Jesus finds her story of personal suffering to ring true to human experience. She has told a remarkable story of survival, and despite what would defeat most others, she has found the faith in humanity to begin loving all over, again and again. Jesus affirms not only the woman's life story as admirable, but her believability and credibility as a person.

No wonder she embodies the ideal evangelist and messenger of good news. No wonder this woman feels energy—her story has been heard and acknowledged by a man who showed deep respect for her. No wonder she feels creative and happy, when she goes back to her relatives and friends, "Come, see a man who told me all I ever did! Can this be the Christ?"

Conclusion

John suggests that an empowering, respectful, one-to-one dialogue is the first act of empowerment, evangelization, and reform. The dialogue of Jesus and the Samaritan is also a model for renewing community life and internal governance structures. Beginning with the one-to-one dialogue, the power of each woman's story is made available to the community, the Church, and the world.

Such a dialogic model also has power to transform: 1) the relation of men to women in the Church; 2) of a leader to each member within a religious community; 3) of religious women to the institutional Church. The model of telling, hearing, asking and answering also provides a direction for how to approach modern culture, despite its alienating features, other faith traditions, political structures, and economic systems thought to be "outside" the fundamental values held by those in consecrated life.

Proposal to the Congress on Religious Life, Rome

That this combined body acknowledge the tragedy of a worldwide, systemic problem, reported by women superiors to the UISG since 1994, about the sexual abuse and exploitation of vowed nuns by male clergy—South America, Africa, Europe, and the U.S.A.

That the Congregation for Institutes of Consecrated Life and Societies of Apostolic Life, in collaboration with the Congregation for the Clergy and the Congregation for Doctrine and Faith promptly publish to all national bodies representing male and female religious the following:

1. The process of administrative recourse whereby the victim herself—novice or professed Sister—may act as petitioner in her own name, bring a complaint and seek redress from the appropriate congregation against the sexual predation, sexual exploitation, or sexual harassment by:

    a. a diocesan priest or deacon

    b. a priest or brother of a religious order.

2. The judicial procedure of seeking redress through a tribunal judgment against a victimizer, by the victim herself, as petitioner in her own name, for sexual predation, sexual exploitation, or sexual harassment by

    a. a diocesan priest or deacon

    b. a priest or brother of a religious order.

3. The administrative procedure by which any Sister dismissed from her congregation after her sexual victimization by a cleric may seek review of her case, and petition for reinstatement in her religious order, or transfer to another religious community.

Exploring the Civil and Canonical Rights of Sisters in Community

1. The Rights of Members

Question: We are preparing for some community education about rights and responsibilities of individual Sisters and of the congregation . . . Several factors have heightened our consciousness of unexplored or changing rights and needs.

Comment: Answers to questions about rights are being shaped in light of the process in which women religious are developing an understanding of themselves as human beings allied with the cause of all other women. A conversational model is needed among theologians, feminists, civil lawyers, canonists, and those with experience of religious life, both leaders and members. There is need for a revolution in thinking, a change in mentality, a paradigm shift from "nun" to "woman."

Some of these issues can be grouped, from the perspective of leadership, around the question, "How shall I deal with the nun who is a problem for me, for the community, or for the sponsored work?" The reality of members' rights has been invisible in the actions leaders take to deal with the "problem Sister." One solution to the community problem has been to make life so difficult for a Sister or to give a personal command in the name of the vow of obedience that is so compromising of her conscience, that she seeks a dispensation from her vows. She typically receives no canonical counsel when she finds herself in anguish over whether to stay or leave. The president, provincial, or prioress may regard canonical advocacy as an intrusion into her personal authority over the congregation and its members.

In dealing with long-term abuses of power, a Sister may "voluntarily" request dispensation, but these departures belong to a category of abuse I would call "constructive dismissal." This is an analogy to the concept in employment law called "constructive termination" where the employer does not actually fire the employee, but makes life on the job so miserable no reasonable employee would stay, and the employee quits. The silence around the abuse of religious power in engineering "constructive dismissals" is an ongoing tragedy and toxification of our community life.

The Sister has lost not just her membership, but her retirement benefits and support in old age. Constructive dismissals are a form not only of social but of economic violence. The question present members should be asking concerns prospective members. Why would any woman enter a religious community when this culture of fear and risk prevails? What control is there over the unilateral power of a superior, typically exercised behind the shield of "confidentiality," and lack of accountability, to "divorce" members from the community, at any stage of their lives? The culture of passivity by which members allow this practice to continue should be shaken out into the light and reformed.

The habit of nonintervention is perhaps inherited from postulant and novitiate days when those who stayed did not question the circumstances of those who departed. However, the conditioning of looking the other way should not prevent finally professed women from challenging the myth that a superior still has authority to dismiss other finally professed members for causes unrelated to serious crimes. Instead of secrecy, there should be accountability and review.

Nonintervention in this secret practice and abuse of authority is a fundamental evil in religious life. The practice itself is as egregious as the sexual abuse of minors. The threat to use such power, which typically takes place behind closed doors, is evidence that religious women remain oppressed by a patriarchal system of power—the unilateral power of the one in authority to take action against the weaker party with no accountability and no review.

Our consciousness needs to be raised from the time when we were postulants and novices—when our companions "disappeared" and we moved up one stall in chapel, neither questioning nor objecting. Today, we still may believe that leadership is entitled to dismiss professed members on "confidential" bases, and the norm for behavior is still the same passive mode of acceptance.

While we reject "blind obedience" as representative of our current spirituality, the old visceral instincts are still affecting the relations of members to leaders. These allow finally professed members to be constructively dismissed on the assumption that when a leader gives a personal directive, she speaks with the authority of Church law. When education about rights begins to challenge this unconscious culture, there will be resistance, upset, and anxiety—because it will feel that religious life is collapsing, or something essential is being lost.

Such a viscerally-felt culture is borne of patriarchal conditioning and ignorance of members' rights. It comes from ignorance of Church teaching about the sacredness of our ecclesial bonds through vows and the safeguards we are entitled to claim. It comes from ignorance of the canonical limits of a superior's personal authority over individual members. It comes from the failure of chapters to establish a governance structure with appellate and review processes that are consistent with the 1983 Code of Canon Law. It comes from an assumption that the vow of obedience somehow attenuates the rights of women under vows to assert the same human and ecclesial rights of the laity that are acknowledged in the code.

The whole matter of "the problem Sister" needs to be taken out of discussions conducted in secret behind closed doors by leaders with a particular member, and by leaders on private telephone calls to canonists.

2. Learnings from Sex Abuse Problems

Question: The recent sex abuse cases have brought weaknesses in Church processes to the fore, such as failure of bishops to address disruptive behavior, overextension of confidentiality to conceal the nature of the problem, and protection of the reputation of the Church or of clerics at the expense of vulnerable victims. Corrective measures caused their own set of problems, such as dismissal of Church personnel without due process, action on allegations even if unsubstantiated, long-term damage to the reputation of innocent Church personnel, and access given to third parties of records that mixed personnel and psychological data.

Comment: The sexual abuse reform, reporting and judicial processes have exposed the mess the Church is in. It also points to how fragile are the structures on which clergy, whether innocent or guilty, have been able to rely. I will simply acknowledge these problems you outline for the moment, but consider the implications for women religious. The fact is that women's ministerial history is not fueling the sex abuse scandal in the way men's is. However, the same governance structure and clerical culture that has contributed to the scandal has also failed to provide a viable means of recourse or due process within the Church for religious women.

Despite forty years since Vatican II, with its affirmation of human rights and promotion of due process, diocesan chanceries are not all on the same page. Discourse about rights of Sisters has to be realistic in light of the lack of structures that acknowledge those rights. No better area than employment in Church-sponsored institutions can be used to illustrate this lack, with no effective dispute-resolution and grievance procedures in parishes and dioceses. However, what structure should exist is an important part of the education in rights. Women religious have the freedom to put structures in place for members, even if they do not exist in chanceries. Vowed women can begin the reform of the Church within our own household.

This area needs a canonist who can explain what Church procedures exist to protect the rights of Sisters. However, canonists, even those who are religious themselves, are unclear on these rights. It is commonly thought that Sisters cannot use tribunals because they belong to pontifical congregations not under the authority of the bishop. This is a false assumption. A Sister has the same rights as a layperson to seek the Church's assistance in resolving disputes. When her own congregation does not provide a viable or fair internal due process procedure, she has a right to seek the local Church's assistance. This is because she enjoys all the rights of the baptized to due process, and because she has made vows in the Church.

This may be liberating information for newer superiors and for members. In the past, a Sister's rights may have been coterminus with the feelings of the superior toward her. The prevailing myth is that if a Sister wishes to appeal a decision or seek review of a superior's directive, she must go to the Congregation for Institutes of Consecrated Life and Societies of Apostolic Life. Such a freedom is in fact so burdensome that it effectively extinguishes a Sister's right to due process. Rank and file members do not know how to contact Rome on their own if they find themselves in a dispute with a regional superior. Further, congregational Constitutions, Directories and Policy Manuals typically make no provision for such occasions. There is no budget line even for seeking canonical counsel. Leadership has access to canonists, but not members.

The existence of diocesan dispute resolution processes should be described. Congregational structures, such as mediation or reconciliation boards, should be activated and members oriented to their function, as part of the education about rights.

3. Employment of Sisters Within Congregationally Sponsored Institutions

Question: Religious communities formerly controlled the placement and evaluation of its members and could reassign Sisters from one congregationally controlled facility to another. For better or worse, the accomplishments and failures of an individual were known only within the congregation. Likewise, a Sister could easily be assigned to a new position without a job interview. Now there is more extensive overlap between congregational missioning and the associated canon law, civil law, and employer regulations involved in many Sisters' ministries.

Comment: For openers, it is my observation that in the congregationally-sponsored employment setting, the rights of a Sister are compromised by the confusion about who she works for. Is the religious superior her boss, or is the CEO of the hospital or principal of the school for example? The net result of this lack of clarity is that the Sister ends up being perceived—by herself and by her institutional supervisors—as not having the rights other employees have to appeal decisions about evaluation or termination.

On the other hand, because she belongs to the sponsoring congregation, she suffers suspicion that she is "privileged" more than other employees. Again, the apologetic posture assumed by the congregation, as if to prove to lay coworkers that Sisters are "no better" than other employees, results in the Sister having no rights either within the institution or within the congregation to protest bad treatment in the workplace. She feels she has no access to grievance structures within the institution, and there are none within the congregation.

A civil lawyer is needed to provide an objective education in what civil law says about employment rights, antidiscrimination legislation and privacy. It will be news to most religious. During the 1960s, they were absorbed in Vatican II documents and renewal of lifestyle and customs within religious life. In those same years, the U.S. was upended by the civil rights movement and the out-pouring of antidiscrimination legislation. The foundational argument about basic human rights which enforced desegregation in the schools, and the connection of racial justice with gender justice, are gaps in the collective awareness and knowledge base of women religious. What happened in public schools in the south was per-ceived as "out there," and not experienced as a movement essen-tially related to the mentality and formation of women religious.

A canon lawyer normally does not have the training to deal with issues of civil law. Most canonists are not trained as theolo-gians, though they do theological work. Some of the issues around the rights of women religious would need to be raised by a review of the Church's teaching on human anthropology, its past and current interpretation of Scripture related to the role of women, compet-ing governance models of the Church in Vatican II documents, the concept of justice for the oppressed, and the spirituality of virtue. Spirituality is not sufficient in itself as an approach to deal with these matters, and in fact, if spirituality controls the language, we might be retarded in the conversation you are proposing. This is because the matter of rights involves social structures and social systems, and the language of spirituality can place the emphasis on the private, personal and interior experience of God. "Rights" is not language associated with the semantics of spirituality.

Unfortunately, civil lawyers and canonists are not always edu-cated to think of nuns as having the same rights as citizens of the U.S. Vows do not abrogate our civil rights. Canonists are some-times confused, and leadership as well, adopting some mythical belief that the vows replace members' secular rights, or that religious have entered into some sort of special zone of "Church" that is separate from "state." Thus, this problem of identity of nuns as women in Church and society is fundamental to the reeducation of nuns, both leaders and members.

Here is where there is need for an updated theology that can reconcile vows and civil rights. This requires a long conversation because it has not been done in Church documents. But the theologian must also disclose in Scripture a revised model of the counsels based on the following of Jesus in the Gospels. If this is not done, the education about civil and canonical rights will be resisted as "empty," "legalistic" and "the laws of the male Church."

There is profound ignorance about the teaching of the Church on rights, as presented in the 1983 Code of Canon Law. Most women in religious life today, and canonists consulted by religious communities, had their religious formation under the 1917 Code. Despite what the Church has taught since, the ideas absorbed in formation have not budged, like childhood faith in what religious life requires of us if we are to be counted faithful.

Not all canonists, civil lawyers or theologians are feminists. As women, we can acknowledge there is a backlash (back to the 1950s Martha Stewart model of house and home) in society and Church. Yet women religious, despite their support of women's ordination, have been conflicted about feminist consciousness for thirty years because a focus on reproductive rights seemed to require a compromise of Catholic moral teaching on abortion. Reframing the commitment to a broader spectrum of women's rights would get around this ethical block.

Women religious need to embrace a more fundamental identification of ourselves with the cause of all women seeking emancipation from theocratic systems, especially those emerging from under the burka in Egypt, Afghanistan, Iraq, and Iran. We should bring to bear our own empathy with what "under the burka" means.

There are some parallels between the international cause of human rights for women and the claiming of our rights as women religious. Thus, the context for these important questions is the international rights of women, not just civil rights in the U.S., or canonical rights in the Church.

4. Employment Rights of Sisters within a Workplace Accountable to Civil Law

Question: It would be helpful to know the civil and canonical rights of Sisters as employees. Many Sisters minister in an environment where there are official employee rights and obligations. How does the congregation and an individual Sister come to terms with her civil employee rights, and congregational rights to "mission" Sisters? What are guiding canonical and civil laws that come to bear on these decisions?

Comment: Leaders and members alike would benefit from being brought up to date about how employment rights of women have been established by federal law and state law. A turning point that recognized the rights of women took place in 1963, with the Equal Pay Act. This was followed by the antidiscrimination provisions of the Civil Rights Act of 1964. A series of laws in the decades since have fundamentally redefined the rights of women in the workplace. However, awareness of these social changes does not seem to have affected the self-understanding of women in religious life in relation to their ministries.

I think it is necessary for the continued renewal of religious life to consider the Sister not only as a religious, but as a citizen. Canonists have not addressed this duality, and their model of the "good Sister" is linked to the virtues instilled in them during their own novitiates prior to Vatican II.

Based on the older model of missioning, or assigning a Sister to work at a particular school or hospital, some theologians tend to think of the Sister as merely an agent or representative of the community. In the view of some diocesan attorneys, she may lack competence to make her own employment contract because the assumption is that only the superior is competent. She has no more rights than those of a minor child. This perception is linked to assumptions about the vow of obedience. Even civil lawyers who advise bishops have failed to articulate the individual rights of Sisters in the workplace. Sisters seem to be a special case, with only those rights as are permitted or authorized by the superior.

This view is based on a mythological concept of religious life as "separation from the world." This creates a substantial need for demythologizing the notion of the Sister as a special case, without the same rights as other women. An assertion must be made that a Sister has the same rights to fair treatment as all other human beings. Both canonists and civil attorneys working for the Church have created problems here for Sisters out of their own ignorance about the dignity and rights of the religious woman.

The reality of this problem should lead religious women to talk with each other about how to solve it. A feminist critique is needed to raise to consciousness the bedrock culture of blind obedience, spirituality based on compliance with the directives of someone else, and a theology of missioning that emphasized virtues that were largely indistinguishable from the social conditioning of women as good wives according to 1950 standards.

Another set of counsels, based on the imitation of Jesus in the Gospels, is needed to replace humility, self-effacement and self-sacrifice unto death—virtues which may have earned Sisters grace in heaven, but have brought them plenty of misery on earth.

Sisters who are vowed members, and also citizens, are entitled to negotiate their own contracts, receive equal pay as laymen, resist unlawful hiring policies, report on deviations from stated policy, appeal bad performance evaluations, sue for sexual harassment and race discrimination, challenge unlawful terminations, and seek damages for all these in both Church and civil forums.

With a few exceptions, Sisters have not asserted their rights as ministers and workers over the last forty years, even when member after member lost her job in a parish or a diocesan office. This has left all religious women quietly conflicted in a love-hate relationship with the institutional Church. Sisters don't know what rights to assert, nor when they can or should, or under what conditions. There are typically no congregational advocates for members to protect and assert their rights in the name of the order. Superiors differ in their policies of supporting or not supporting the rights of members in the workplace from one administrative term to another. There is no policy, and no thought about such policy that appears on any congregational agenda or chapter of affairs, to my knowledge.

When a Sister is an employee in the congregation's sponsored works, and experiences unfair treatment by a lay administrator, the matter of asserting her rights becomes complicated and touchy. Her oppression, as an inability to assert her rights, is demonstrated by her lack of access to an advocate in human resources, the shadow of the superior who doesn't want her to create trouble, the ambiguity of whether she works for the religious superior or works for the institution, and the turning of Sisters against each other within the institution. These dynamics have a disillusioning and fragmenting effect on Sisters' relations with each other.

The silence and avoidance of the issue of Sisters' rights in congregational institutions does not promote effective sponsorship. How Sisters treat each other establishes a norm for how lay administrators feel entitled to treat lay employees.

5. Rights to Confidentiality in Psychological and Psychiatric Services.

Question: Dealing with the rights to confidentiality in psychological services creates a number of dilemmas for congregations. Congregations expect access to psychological records as a prerequisite to membership. Beyond initial formation, leadership may look to psychological evaluations to help determine if a member has a serious illness.

Comment: This matter needs not so much a canonist as someone with knowledge of the laws that govern psychological counseling. Consultations with psychiatrists and psychologists involve state law about privacy of medical records, and the laws vary from state to state in the U.S. A good resource would be a civil lawyer who can explain privacy rights under civil law. How psychological testing and medical exams are handled in employment settings offers one paradigm to compare and contrast with the fuzziness of policies within religious community about confidentially of medical records and psychological reports.

A canonical discussion needs to be informed by what civil law says. Sending a vowed member from the U.S. to a treatment center in Canada, for example, compromises the right a Sister has to privacy in her counseling relationship under U.S. law. A Sister who goes outside the country for psychological treatment waives the rights she would have in the U.S. and in her own state. She agrees that a religious superior will receive the psychological reports. In effect, a member is treated as incompetent or like a minor child whose "parent," the superior, pays for treatment and "takes charge" of the member's healthcare. A superior, by virtue of her office, has no inherent right to "take charge" and intrude into the conscience of a member without the free choice of the member. A member in this situation has the right to name her own representative, even if it is not the superior. She also has a right to refuse treatment.

When leadership decides a member should get counseling to "straighten herself out," i.e., because she doesn't approve of a member's attitude or behavior, and the issue does not concern criminal behavior, substance abuse, or conduct that is a danger to herself or others, a member is not required to disclose anything about her counseling to a superior, simply because the superior signs the checks for the counseling.

It is interrelational violence for a superior to coerce a Sister to go to therapy by threatening to take away her car, withhold her budget check, or force her to leave her living situation unless she complies. Unfortunately, I am aware of Sisters who have been subjected to this kind of treatment. None of the reasons that prompted the threat by the superior were genuine health emergencies. A member has the right to refuse counseling in such an instance, and to call leadership to accountability through a review process. But review processes do not presently exist to protect members from this sort of abuse of authority.

In the matter of admission of members to the congregation, leadership does have the right to inquire thoroughly into the background of a candidate. It is analogous to the security clearance that must be obtained by persons seeking employment with some federal agencies, such as the Federal Bureau of Investigation or the Central Intelligence Agency. Some professions, such as law, also require extensive background checks to verify personal recommendations, establish citizenship, ascertain residence, review educational and employment history, certify marital status and name changes, verify records of hospitalizations for mental illness, treatment for drug and alcohol addiction, bankruptcies, criminal arrests and prosecutions, and any professional disciplinary history. These are appropriate inquiries also into the background of candidates for religious life.

However, religious communities need to have a secure depository, and a clear privacy policy about what happens to such records. Which persons will be qualified to receive and review them? Since leadership changes with each term's election, and not all Sisters elected to office have the same professional qualifications, there needs to be a policy that protects a member from too broad an access to her records. Another question is at what point to destroy records that served as the basis for making a decision about entrance and acceptance for first profession.

If a member is refused admission or acceptance into the novitiate on the basis of such records, there needs to be a policy—not the choice of an individual superior—about what to tell her. Once she is accepted to first profession, and she is refused advancement several years later to final profession on the basis of "going back" to these records, she has in my view an absolute right to defend herself against the allegations she is unfit, and to seek review of this decision at the highest level of the congregation, as well as in ecclesial forums.

6. Stewardship of Community Resources

Question: How does a congregation balance the individual's right to counseling services and confidentiality with the stewardship of resources?

Comment: Religious communities have spent hundreds of thousands of dollars on counseling for members in the last decades. Sometimes the cost of these private, supportive conversations is increased because there is no place within the structure of community life for a Sister to address systemic abuses of power that caused her to lose her parish or diocesan job when "father" fired her. There is no ministry advocate to go to bat for her. There is no place on the congregational agenda to acknowledge that the loss of Church-related employment is a congregational issue, not a Sister's personal loss of a job.

We have created our own financial stewardship problem, in part, because of the reflex which directs a Sister who lost a job and suffered trauma, "See your spiritual director to find peace with God, and see your therapist to deal with your anger." This is the message to scores of Sisters. It has had a financial impact on our congregations. A rather hard-nosed comment I heard from one Sister-advisor to other religious congregation was, "Membership in a religious community does not entitle a Sister to a lifetime of therapy." The speaker seemed to regard the member as a private, self-indulgent consumer of costly psychological services who needed to toughen up and stop draining the congregation's treasury.

An important matter concerns counseling for members who are survivors of childhood sexual abuse and adult sexual exploitation. The statistics for women religious mirror that of society at large. About 20 percent are survivors of childhood sexual trauma. About 10 percent of members at large report adult experience of sexual exploitation and harassment. This means that about one quarter of our membership bears heavy burdens just from this source of trauma.

A discussion about how much the congregation pays for psychological services, and how much a member deserves, masks the deeper problem that a significant proportion of our membership bears terrible pain that has not been addressed as a systemic form of suffering unique to women—a universal experience of sexual, physical, emotional, financial, and legal violence. We should challenge superiors who put the question as merely a financial matter of stewardship of common resources. If they knew their members' stories better, and were more empathetic to the suffering of women as a gender, they might change the way they approach the matter of counseling.

My thought is that any Sister who is using psychological services for a long time, and still cannot find healing, has not found peace because her community has not been part of the healing process. It has made her the problem by posing it as a stewardship issue. The mentality of the community continually rewounds a member when it blames her for spending the community's money, yet does not acknowledge that she is a bearer of the community's ills, and women's ills as a class. The mission of many women's congregations includes a commitment to relieve the misery of the oppressed and poor. These include the members of religious communities themselves.

If congregations were more committed to seek justice for their members, rejoicing that women stood up for themselves after being violated as children, or treated unjustly as employees, and providing the professional support to do so, there might be less need for creating these gulags in which professional counseling may be the only forum to tell someone their story. By "gulag" I mean a member feels isolated and punished for seeking counseling and "costing the community so much."

The community typically provides no forum for claiming these experiences as part of the congregation's revered history of their own members overcoming adversity. Members are expected to work out their problems secretly on their own, sparing the community the burden of their stories, as though these personal issues had nothing to do with the physical and sexual victimization of women as a gender, and the systemic injustice and inequality of women in Church and society.

7. Right to a Good Name

Question: Many factors contribute to a history of secrecy in religious life, the desire to keep confidentiality, hierarchical structure, or preservation of reputation. Unfortunately, the overextension of those values has led to unexplained transfers, incomplete communications, and a sense of mistrust when unfavorable, but unexamined allegations are made. What rights does a Sister have to know the source and content of allegations brought against her?

Comment: The right to a good name is a two-edged concept in the Church. Canon 220 affirms the right of believers to protect their good name. However, in the context of the sexual abuse crisis, with clergy accused, and now prosecuted for their crimes against minors, protection of clerics' good name yields to demand for accountability to society. Formerly, the reputation of a clergy-predator was protected by invoking his right to a good name despite an allegation against him. Bishops asserted their right to administer the discipline of clergy without interference from the state into internal matters of Church governance.

The Church made sexual abuse a sin that could be forgiven in the confessional, not a crime that had to be accounted for to society.

Typically in a women's community, confidentiality is used lovingly, to protect members from embarrassment and loss of respect. There is no publication of a Sister's auto accident, for example. On the other hand, confidentiality has been cited to forestall accountability of leadership to members, and prevent public discussion of the circumstances leading a professed member to leave the community when she reports that her canonical rights were not acknowledged and there was lack of due process or any access to a review. In this case, confidentiality is being abused.

Profession of first vows bestows a right on a member to be secure in her commitment to God. The Church grants her the greater freedom—to leave if she discerns the life is not for her. However, after first profession, the Church restricts the freedom of superiors to unilaterally dismiss her prior to final profession. An individual superior should not be allowed by the membership to act privately in this matter on her own authority, using "confidentiality" as a shield, to overturn the affirmation of those who previously confirmed the Sister's vocation.

If the superior makes such a decision, it is not confidential, but subject to an open review and the accountability of an appellate process. That means the superior's reasons must be in writing so that others in higher authority may read what she thinks and why. The member has a right to defend herself and counter the judgment that she is unfit by offering her own evidence from her own supporters and have this matter reviewed through an impartial process.

A woman admitted and approved by one leadership team, then found "unsuitable" by a Sister later elected to leadership, has a right to appeal that decision. While there is no "right" to make final profession, there is a right to be treated fairly and judged using objective criteria. It is a woman's human and ecclesial right to defend herself against accusations that she is not suitable for final profession. Just so, a member who suffers from other members' accusations or comes into conflict with a superior later in life and is threatened with dismissal has an absolute right to seek an open forum in which to defend herself. Such disciplinary actions are not to be done in private.

This ecclesial right is comparable to the civil rights enshrined is in the U.S. Constitution's Sixth Amendment guaranteeing all citizens the right to publicly confront their accusers, and to have a public trial—accessible to the general public. There is a demand in a democratic society that judgments about an a person's wrongdoing will be subject to fair, objective judicial procedures in which there is impartial process made based on law and evidence. These values run exactly counter to the culture of "confidentiality" in religious life, which has allowed abuses of authority, such as lack of accountability in disciplinary actions taken against members, to flourish in secret.

The culture of women's religious life needs to be reexamined about its use and abuse of confidentiality. The custom of the Jesuits permits secret letters to be sent to the provincial about someone nominated for congregational office. The nominee is not informed about these communications. The provincial can consider these letters in making his decision.

However, such a practice is alien to the concept of American civil rights. Every U.S. citizen is guaranteed due process, the right to make a defense against allegations of crime or wrongdoing, and to have assistance of an advocate. A person has the right to openly confront those who have made accusations. When such a right is denied to terrorists who are confined under U.S. military control and held incommunicado for months, alert citizens are concerned at the violation of basic democratic principles.

The hierarchical structure of religious life has not been examined for its compliance with Church teaching that protects the right of defense. Besides the top-down structure, there needs to be a down-up appellate structure clearly in place by which members can appeal up the line to higher authority, and be provided a procedure to clear their name by challenging the evidence lodged against them in secret.

In the old culture of obedience, members did not presume to assert their rights. They complied with what they were told to do. They lacked competence, it was presumed, to make personal decisions, or to defend themselves against false accusations without leave from a superior. This was supposed to be the practice of humility and acceptance of the Cross by members. Since they did not send themselves into service to a particular school or hospital, they also lacked competence to assert that injustice was done to them as employees. If they were talked about, they enjoyed no process to defend themselves. Superiors had the right to talk about "subjects" but Sisters themselves were not invited to be part of that conversation going on over their heads. They were regarded as children or as chairs.

Vowed members are generally illiterate about their human, civil, and ecclesial rights, and like women deprived of education under the Taliban, they must start with the basics of the justice alphabet, as it were. There is a system of formative spirituality in religious life that has reinforced this ignorance and made the lack of knowledge itself a virtue.

8. Coercion and Undue Influence

Question: *Even when a Sister has canonical or civil rights, she may believe she must relinquish those rights because of the stated or implied expectation of the vow of obedience or virtue of humility toward the superior, the Sister's own understanding of obedience or humility, or fear of long-term consequences of social exclusion, diminished voice in congregational matters or compromised reputation. What information can help allay those understandings?*

Comment: The rights of Sisters as baptized persons should be the starting point. The theological rhetoric has focused on the sacramental assertion that vows are the continuation of baptism. What is needed is a reflection on the fact that women in vows have the same rights to due process and fair treatment as laity.

However, canonists who are members of religious orders are confused when it comes to the vow of obedience. Obedience as submission to the will of the superior is so ingrained that an attempt to examine whether this premise is sufficient or reasonable meets resistance. Religious life seems to be a "special case" or exception in which the vow of obedience trumps basic human rights, ecclesial rights and civil rights. Compromise the vow of obedience, and religious life will fall apart, seems the supposition. Rights in the Church are for everyone except women in vows. Women in religious life have internalized their own oppression.

Language about rights seems so alien that they resist these concepts as, ironically, the imposition of patriarchal values.

There is presently profound ignorance about the dignity of the person as that principle applies to vowed women. Feminist consciousness-raising of the last forty years has had little impact on the internal culture of religious life. There should be an examination why. After a brief period of enlightenment following Vatican II, women in religious life lost the light about their entitlements to due process. There has been no continuity in communal memory of these post-Vatican II insights. Aging members also suffer malaise, depression, and fatigue; the light has failed them.

Sisters might profitably ask themselves questions about what they are entitled to do, and what they might do in each of these situations if they were laypeople: What if they were dismissed from a Church-related job? sexually exploited by a priest? embarrassed by several people reading their medical records? defamed by a coworker so that friends turn away from them? forced by relatives to have medical tests and procedures they don't want? If there is any question that a woman in vows would not have the same right to assert herself as does a layperson, what are the dynamics in the culture of religious life that impose these limitations?

The traditional holiness code suggests a woman in vows should "develop virtue," which generally translates as a directive that she is not to assert herself, her preferences, or her feelings of outrage. She is not supposed to care how she is treated.

Actually, much of the holiness code for women is simply socialization of women to make a virtue of their second-class status in Church and society. Some justify their lack of rights by appealing to their "call to follow Jesus." The less assertive she is, and the more self-effacing, the more like Jesus she is. However, this is a self-defeating code. It might be part of the reason healthy women in society do not feel attracted to religious life.

If there is to be a viable and vital future for religious life, all these questions you have posed need to be explored more fully.

Why an Appeals Process Is Important for Our West-Mid-West Governance Model

I t would be useful to imagine our new governance structure open to some possibilities that reflect Vatican II's encouragement forty years ago that religious communities of women update their constitutions and lifestyles. An important part of *aggiornamento* has not yet been achieved by the Sisters of Mercy—the incorporation of a viable due process structure and internal appeals process that protect the rights of members to review decisions that aggrieve them and defend themselves against accusations brought against them by other members. The Church protects the rights of laity (or is supposed to) through its judicial structure. Our reconciliation process is seriously flawed in its assumptions and procedure. It cannot work either to appeal decisions or to reconcile disputes, given the conditions that were attached to it in 1991.

After Vatican II, there were a number of important studies of the rights of the laity, including religious. I summarized some of these in an article I wrote in the *MAST Journal* 14. No 2 (2004) "The Reconciliation Process: An Ecclesial Structure for Protecting Rights of Members," pp 20–41. For the orientation of Reconciliation Board members sponsored by the Institute Women's Commission in March 2005, Sr. Lois Keller, R.S.M. (Brooklyn) outlined the rights of Sisters of Mercy in a 2005 brochure.

Mission to the Oppressed: A Source for Grasping the Concept of Rights

The concept of "rights" is a term we associate with our international justice perspective, such as the right of migration, the right to clean water, the right to education, the right to express divergent views in speech and press, the right to vote and exercise democratic choice of one's own political leaders.

For Mercies, the concept of human rights is especially compelling because we remember Catherine McAuley's commitment to protect poor women's right to safe living accommodations, a woman's right to respectful care when she was sick or old, the right to decent working conditions for women free of sexual exploitation, the right of girls to education and the right of women to practice their own faith without sacrificing any of their other entitlements as citizens in Ireland.

As religious women focused on ministry to the poor and oppressed in society, we can feel assured remembering that we also have a commitment to each other to affirm and protect the rights of our Sisters as vowed women. In the Church, women with vows enjoy the rights of laity because baptism is the sacrament of our equality; our vows do not take away the rights to justice and fair treatment that laity have. Within our congregational governance structure, we have the added protection of the Church as vowed women—or should have.

I am urging the WMW Governance Group to consider thoughtfully the commitment we have to affirm and protect the rights of our own Sisters as vowed women. This theme may seem new. However, it only feels strange because it has not been part of our discourse since Vatican II. Rome is partly to blame, because no documents on religious life have treated this theme of protection of the rights of vowed members. There is also theological confusion about the vow of obedience. Doesn't the right of a superior to command obedience take precedence over a member's rights of appeal, defense, and canonical counsel? Doesn't the vow of obedience demand a member's sacrifice of her right to due process? Isn't submission to a superior's decision a greater virtue than asserting her right to be treated fairly? The short answer to all these is: No.

Public Exercise of Leadership vs. Acts Behind Closed Doors with Individuals

These issues do not arise so much in the public exercise of leadership in Mercy. In public, the issue is participation of members in governance, and the frequency and quality of participation are publicly measured. However, the matter of rights is critical in taking account of *private* acts where leaders assert their authority over

101

members in one-on-one interchanges where there is no public accountability. Behind closed doors, at meetings where members are summoned, interchanges go on in secret, as in the days of our novitiate, when the novice director called us into her office.

This private, "off the grid" situation is where some regional leaders have felt entitled to make decisions to deny Sisters in first profession approval to proceed to final profession. It is evident that we presently have no review process to test the objectivity and fairness of such a decision. A proposal to have such a process was presented, though not acted upon at the last Chapter.

I would urge the Governance Work Group to image governance possibilities outside the closed system of our previous experience of religious life. There are some new concepts—the conviction that members have inalienable human rights—that could meaningfully affect governance structure reform.

Importance of the Conversation Model of Governance

In responding to the Governance Paper, I think the "conversation" model is more workable for a governance structure than a "gospel friendship" theme. Dialogue and its preservation are the soul of a healthy marriage, and critical for sustaining relations among adult women in religious life. What structures will assure dialogue continuing, even in the face of human reluctance to do the work needed to repair relations?

At the present time, I don't think our governance structures are prophetic because they do not include a "balance of powers" that guarantees dialogue at all levels. We have a legislative process (Chapters) and executive structures (RLT, ILC, ILT), but no independent judicial or appellate structure. If the dialogic process between leaders and members breaks down, there is no structure, such as an appellate process, that provides—by mandating it—a continuation of the conversation. There are presently no viable structures to appeal decisions that feel retaliatory or discriminatory.

What about the personalized decision by a leader that is well-intentioned, but lacks full information, deviates from Church or civil law, is arbitrary, or differs from what a superior in a different region would do? What place can any individual Sister or group go within Mercy to seek an impartial review or a reconciliation process to heal breaches of charity? Where is the process to anneal old hurts or ease on-going grudges that belie "the sun never went down on their anger" ? A viable appeals process and a revised reconciliation process are sorely needed. Where are right relations for each other?

Cultural Tension in Religious Life: Democracy vs. Theocracy

I see our present governance structures affected by a cultural conflict between theocracy and democracy that impedes our flourishing. Part of the culture controlling the religious life of women is patriarchal and theocratic. We are familiar with political structures in Afghanistan and Iran that are theocracies. God's authority is invoked as the basis for political power.

As we see in the middle east, theocracies select mullahs, the most devout men, as political leaders, and a theocracy typically exercises absolute power over all aspects of Islamic private and public life. A theocracy under the Taliban exercised that power by subjecting women to a domestic life at home, denying girls schooling and forbidding them to work, vote, or appear unveiled in public—all in the name of religious observance.

Typically, women in a theocracy lack the same human rights as men because they are not regarded as persons with the same dignity and equality. There is no appeal from the decision of the mullahs who are at the same time political leaders and judges who apply religious law. Women must simply submit or risk death. It is a closed system and not a democracy.

If we do the analysis of authority in religious life of women, we would first acknowledge that we live in a special kind of theocracy—God is the most important dimension of our lives. Surely this is intended to be a benevolent theocracy where the gospel is our inspiration. We choose leaders to carry out the mission we understand we have from God. Our internal governance is inspired by religious principles. We choose women we expect to embody our faith and values.

However, it is inevitable that within our own theocracy, some of the dynamics of modern political theocracies can manifest themselves. I see this in the conflict between a democratic rhetoric (participative governance) on one hand and, on the other, the "handing down" of policies on occasion that have not been discussed or affirmed by the vote of members at large.

There are clear Constitutional provisions for preserving a democratic right to choose our own leadership, but not a structure of accountability for members to seek review for the decisions leaders make about them. There is no process by which members defend themselves against accusations made by third parties. Thus, I see a conflict between democratic principles of organization and theocratic practices in Mercy governance. One evidence is that despite our claim to be a democracy, we lack a structure that guarantees democratic values: an independent judiciary or review process.

Western democracies balance the tendency of governments to exercise too much power over citizens by having a "check and balance" structure. This is served in part by having an independent judicial structure. In religious life, *aggiornamento* would be fostered by a review process. An appellate structure would insure the continuation of our democratic and participative governance structure. This would also more faithfully mirror the Church's own tradition of a judicial branch that guarantees, at least on the books, a fair hearing to both sides. At the same time, we also admit that having a judicial branch does not thereby guarantee democratic governance within the Church!

As exercised by women religious, however, an appellate process would be a prophetic structure within our congregational life. Even political theocracies have judicial structures—where the mullahs interpret religious law as it applies to disputes among members. Mercy is impoverished, both as a theocracy and as a democracy, by lacking a viable internal review process where decisions, policies and directives are tested against the Constitutions and Church teaching. This need is not satisfied by leadership calling on canonists for advice on how to deal with a particular situation. A canonist does not replace a permanent governance structure accessible to all members.

Commitment to Dialogue as the Paradigm for Resolving Disputes
I support how the WMW governance paper describes congregational relationships within a horizontal model, ideally more like a

healthy marriage of equals where the one partner does not unilaterally "boss" another. In a good marriage, power sharing has to be worked out on the basis of a contractual relationship. This model may offer a way out of the parental history that informs relations between religious superiors and members.

The possibilities of the dialogue and conversation model would be enhanced by structures that insure dialogue will go on even when leaders are frustrated with this or that member, or dialogue between members breaks down. When dialogue breaks down, or tensions arise, the tendency in any social group is to handle the situation by violence, by imposing a unilateral decision, the silent treatment, or separation of individuals physically from one another. In families, there are no legal rules that compel the overcoming of splits, arguments or hurts, only the conviction of members that families should try to live in harmony. Grudges are held as long as family members choose to keep them.

However, religious community is not a family without a rudder, without a means to structure a process toward forgiveness, resolution of disputes, and restoration of communication. Mercies are blessed with gospel ideals, our foundress's charism, our Constitutions and the Church's canonical provisions. However, these must be translated into structures that assure justice is as much an internal governance principle as a ministerial theme.

Church teaching, and the principles of the reconciliation process provide remedies when conversation about congregational decision making breaks down, leaders do not talk to members, or members do not talk with each other. Church law provides processes, whether it is specifically mentioned in the Constitutions or not. A religious community is an ecclesial body incorporated within the community of faith. At the same time, women of Mercy can choose structures by which to govern themselves. This is why I urge the choice and provision of a genuine appellate process within our governance structure.

Review Guarantee Dialogue to Safeguard Members' Rights

A review process serves many practical purposes on the eve of WMW re-organization, when we know we will be part of a community where we don't know most of the members. It is inevitable that decision making in the near future will be made by leaders and committees who do not have a relational history with the persons whom they represent in leadership.

In such a moment, the provision of a review process is simply good sense. Decision making should have safeguards that insure that the conversation about any member is fully informed with the facts and reasonably shielded from bias or arbitrary standards. Most importantly, such a process mandates that leaders must hear a member's own side of the story when she is the one being discussed by leaders above her and they are making decisions about her in consultation only with each other.

Religious women without a viable appellate process are presently about fifty years out of date. Most religious congregations have a long way to go in adopting post-Vatican II provisions for due process, so Mercy is not unique. Given Mercy charism, it would seem timely that the WMW Governance work group do some spade work and help Mercy catch up with U.S. society, where women's access to fair treatment has been guaranteed for citizens by many changes in the law since the 1970s.

Mercy could begin with the catch-up by formally affirming the rights of the baptized and appropriating the reforms codified in the 1983 Code of Canon Law regarding due process. I believe this would make Mercy more credible to women in society who might consider religious life. Without reforming our internal governance structures, we appear to endorse the same social values for women associated with 1950s housewives from *Father Knows Best*.

This discussion about the importance of grievance procedures and an appellate structure within our governance model is absolutely essential to the revitalization of religious life. U.S. democracy got it right—separation of the powers of executive, legislative, and judicial. We should think about how this could be reflected in our new configuration.